EDUCATION IN
SUB-SAHARAN AFRICA

REFERENCE BOOKS IN
INTERNATIONAL EDUCATION
(General Editor: Edward R. Beauchamp)
(VOL. 11)

GARLAND REFERENCE LIBRARY
OF SOCIAL SCIENCE
(VOL. 576)

Reference Books in International Education

Edward R. Beauchamp
General Editor

EDUCATION IN
SUB-SAHARAN AFRICA
A Source Book

George E.F. Urch

GARLAND PUBLISHING, INC. • NEW YORK & LONDON
1992

Library of Congress Cataloging-in-Publication Data

Urch, George E. F.
  Education in Sub-Saharan Africa : a source book / George E. F. Urch.
    p.   cm. — (Garland reference library of social science ; vol.
  576. Reference books in international education ; vol. 11)
  Includes bibliographical references and index.
  ISBN 0-8240-8444-6 (alk. paper)
    1. Education—Africa, Sub-Saharan. I. Title. II. Series:
Garland reference library of social science ; v. 576. III. Series:
Garland reference library of social science. Reference books in
international education ; vol. 11.
LA1501.U73   1992   91-33314
370'.967—dc20   CIP

Printed on acid-free, 250-year-life paper
Manufactured in the United States of America

To Dorothy and George, Vanessa and Craig

CONTENTS

SERIES EDITOR'S FOREWORD

This series of scholarly works in comparative and international education has grown well beyond the initial conception of a collection of reference books. Although retaining its original purpose of providing a resource to scholars, students, and a variety of other professionals who need to understand the role played by education in various societies or regions of the world, it also strives to provide up-to-date information on a wide variety of selected educational issues, problems and experiments within an international context.

Contributors to this series are well-known scholars who have devoted their professional lives to the study of their specialization. Without exception these men and women possess an intimate understanding of the subject of their research and writing. Without exception they have not only studied their subject in dusty archives, but they have also lived and travelled widely in their quest for knowledge. In short, they are "experts" in the best sense of that often overused word.

In our increasingly interdependent world, it is now widely understood that it is a matter of survival that we not only understand better what makes other societies tick, but that we also make a serious effort to understand how others, be they Japanese, German or Chilean, attempt to solve the same kinds of educational problems that we face in North America. As the late George Z.F. Bereday wrote: "[E]ducation is a mirror held against the face of a people. Nations may put on blustering shows of strength to conceal public weakness, erect grand facades to conceal shabby backyards, and profess peace while secretly arming for conquest, but how they take care of their children tells unerringly who they are" (*Comparative Method in Education*, New York: Holt, Rinehart & Winston, 1964, p. 5).

Perhaps equally important, however, is the valuable perspective that studying another education system (or its problems) provides us in understanding our own system (or its problems). To step outside of our own limited experience and our commonly held assumptions about schools and learning in order to look back at our system in contrast to another places it in a very different light. To learn, for example, how the Soviet Union or Belgium handle the education of a multilingual society; how the French provide for the funding of public education; or how the Japanese control admissions into their universities enables us to understand that there are alternatives to our own familiar way of doing things. Not that we can often "borrow" directly from other societies; indeed, educational arrangements are inevitably a reflection of deeply rooted political, economic and cultural factors that are unique to a society. But a conscious recognition that there are other ways of doing things can serve to open our minds and provoke our imaginations in ways that can result in new approaches that we would not have otherwise considered.

Since this series is intended to be a useful research tool, the editor and contributors welcome suggestions for future volumes as well as ways in which this series can be improved.

Edward R. Beauchamp
University of Hawaii

ACKNOWLEDGMENTS

A volume of this kind requires the help of many people and I have sought assistance from a wide range of sources. The opportunity to work and travel in Africa has given me the privilege to discuss issues with educational leaders. Their experiences have helped me to form questions and concerns. My colleagues and students at the University of Massachusetts Center for International Education have provided me with insights and led me to new resources. They have given me an academic community that enriches my learning environment.

The early research assistance of Elizabeth Paddy was most appreciated. Sally Dumont and Tracie Donohoe helped with the typing of early drafts. Their cooperation was special. Peggy Louraine put the manuscript into its final form. Her knowledge of word processing and attention to detail helped with a smooth transition to a final product.

I would especially like to acknowledge, with gratitude, the editorial assistance of Dorothy M. Urch, my wife. Her task was often tedious and her rewards slight. Her careful reading and commenting on the manuscript and her thoughtful questions guided my thinking.

Finally, I would like to acknowledge Ed Beauchamp for his support throughout the project. I knew he was always there to be helpful.

The mistakes in judgment, of course, are my own. I alone am responsible for what is said here.

PREFACE

The purpose of this volume is to present an overview of recent educational developments on the African continent. A description of the current educational situation in each principal country is followed by commentary on available reference material needed for further investigation. Quite often educational developments relate to national directions charted by policy makers who view the schools as a vehicle to help attain national goals. As a consequence, the book also provides a view of national aspirations on a continent with diverse cultures in a state of rapid change.

The book is arranged in chapters by geographical regions -- West, Central, East, Southern and South. The region South refers to the Republic of South Africa. Background information on regional developments is followed by a summary of educational policy and practice for every major country within the region. This descriptive material provides an overview of educational progress in each nation; as well as an exploration of the educational structure and how the system functions.

Each chapter is further subdivided into subjects for which an annotated bibliography is prepared. The subjects include: history and philosophy; education and development; primary education; secondary education; tertiary and higher education; specialized education (adult, community, nonformal, technical, vocational); curriculum and methods; teachers; religion and private education; and education for women. Bibliographies and references to policy and administration are listed under the subject of education and development.

The introductory section contains a short essay that examines those contemporary educational issues and concerns which transcend single subjects and national boundaries. It also contains a synopsis of research on education in Sub-Saharan Africa. The annotated bibliographic sections in each region list books, journal articles and some published reports of major governmental and international organizations. Not included are newspaper articles, dissertations and locally published reports. Guides to North American dissertations already are available and local reports are difficult to obtain. The journals cited are those usually found in North America or, in some instances, Great Britain. The range of journals help to familiarize the reader with the kind that contain articles on African education. The concluding section contains a list of journals that regularly publish articles on African education.

By definition the bibliography is selective in several ways. Only material written in English is included. This excludes a body of literature written in European languages, especially in French, and a growing body of literature written in African languages. However, in most parts of the continent the bulk of the research on education is published in English. The time frame also is selective. In an attempt to be current only those books and reports written during the past two decades (1970-1990) are included. Journal articles only are included if they were published in the past decade (1980-1990). Reference is made to earlier works in the introductory section on research where well known seminal works and highly respected authors are noted.

The subjects chosen to emphasize also help make the bibliography selective. While the subjects are fairly inclusive of most everything written, a few topics are excluded. These include topical references to some social science research where passing comments on education are made. In any bibliography an important factor in selecting references is what is available. For example in West Africa, Nigeria, with a population of over 120 million people, produces a great deal more written material than some countries that have not yet developed their research potential. In other geographical areas, where English is the third or fourth language, little is available. The subject matter also dictates availability. Many publications come from people in universities, who tend to focus on that aspect of education they know best, namely higher education. On the other hand, there is a noticeable lack of written material on women in education.

Virtually all books and reports annotated were reviewed by the author. University and college libraries were explored in North America to determine availability. The library at the University of London School of Oriental and African Studies also was utilized. In compiling the journal articles, liberal use was made of the ERIC system as well as those core journals known for their emphasis on comparative and international education.

While the bibliography is selective, it also can be viewed as a reasonable comprehensive collection of the most recent and important literature available on education in Sub-Saharan Africa. In many ways it is the most complete available resource for scholars and researchers and can be used as a guide to literature in the field.

INTRODUCTION

Major Problems in African Education

As African political leaders and educators prepare to meet the last decade of the twentieth century, there are some persistent concerns which face formal education throughout the continent. These concerns can be found in five overarching and often interrelated areas. They are: (1) the African heritage, what to retain, modify, or replace; (2) the colonial heritage; (3) the language problem in the schools; (4) the dichotomy between education for self-reliance vs. education for technological and industrial advancement; and (5) education for national unity. This short essay will explore these five themes in light of the experiences gained in the development of education over the past thirty years.

The African Heritage: What to Retain, to Modify or Replace

Across the continent, educators are seriously reviewing what can be retained of their cultural heritage and how the schools can help in this process. After independence, political expediency necessitated an expansion of the educational system inherited from the metropolitan power. However, the new leaders soon realized that their cultural tradition provided a needed social cohesion. During the colonial period Western oriented education often divorced students from their culture and moved them toward a different life style. Often this life style led to a rapid social disintegration of ethnic communities, the dysfunctionality of traditional family life, a refusal by the youth to return to the land, and a rise in delinquency and crime.

In a desire to deal with these problems and develop social stability in the face of rapid change, the new leaders turned to the schools. Education was viewed as a vehicle to promote what was best in the African heritage. The challenge was to determine what should be introduced into the educational system. Needed was that part of African tradition which would regenerate social unity and promote what was good and respected in the culture. Such a tradition would assert the rights and interests of the people, help to reject foreign ideologies and provide a foundation for continuity. It also would promote what was unique in the African personality.

However, while searching for those unique qualities, African educators were aware of the danger in keeping emotionally alive a traditional system that was inadequate for the modern world. In some instances charges were made about a harkening back to the

1

"good old days" rather than coming to terms with modernity.

One individual who offered concrete examples of how to utilize the African heritage in a modern educational system was Julius K. Nyerere, the former President of Tanzania. Nyerere saw the system inherited from the colonial power as an elitist system which divorced the youth from their society and engendered the belief that all worthwhile knowledge was acquired from books and educated people. The new role education was to foster was outlined in his "Education for Self-Reliance" manifesto (Nyerere: 1968). Nyerere stated that education must prepare young people for the work they will be called upon to do in the society which exists -- a rural society where improvement would depend upon the efforts of the people in agriculture and in village development. The schools had to foster the social goals of living and working together for the common good. This meant they must emphasize cooperative endeavors, not individual advancement. They must also stress concepts of equality and the responsibility to give service; and in particular the schools must counteract the temptation toward intellectual arrogance.

Another author, who has discussed the need to retain the best in African tradition, was A. Babs Fafunwa. Fafunwa stated that in traditional African society the purpose of education was clear. The guiding principle was functionalism. In particular, education must emphasize social responsibility, job orientation, political participation and spiritual and moral values (Fafunwa, 1982, p. 9). What was less clear was how these features translated into the curriculum of a modern African school system.

The challenge to retain and incorporate the best of African tradition in the modern classroom still remains. Most nations have a philosophical stance which emphasizes the need and some nations have curriculum material which addresses it. However, the colonial heritage remains and directly relates to what is taught and what is learned. All nations recognize this -- some are attempting to do something about it.

The Colonial Heritage

African leaders today are faced with the task of reevaluating and reshaping those institutions imposed on them by the former colonial power. One such institution is education for these emerging nations have inherited a formal educational structure not linked to the realities of present African needs.

For most nations the political colonial experience began with the Berlin Conference of 1884 and ended in the 1960's with independence. Until the 1950's only two independent sub-Saharan African states existed -- Ethiopia and Liberia. However, contact with Europeans took place long before the Berlin Conference. For formal education this primarily meant missionaries, who had begun to penetrate the continent by the start of the twentieth century.

Education was seen by most missionaries as an essential part of evangelism and they established schools soon after they arrived. To propagate the faith meant that the African had to learn to read and write, for literacy was necessary to understand the scripture and spread it to others. In carrying out their mission the missionaries did not always recognize the traditional religious and cultural values. Instead they were apt to sweep aside things African and replace them with their own Western values. Before long the schools were dominated by a Western-styled literary education. This is what the missionary-educators understood and this is what they taught.

When colonial governments began to establish tighter controls over their subjects, they saw the need to support the missions in their effort to promote religion and European values. However, they also saw the need for the schools to prepare African youth for service to the colonial government and to the economic interests of the European trader. In some cases this meant a form of trade or industrial education. Divergent thought between the colonial governments and various mission denominations over the role of education led to different educational policies in different colonies. Whatever the policy, there was always a consistent and conscious effort to educate Africans away from their culture (Fafunwa: 1982, p. 21).

Often the African student was the hapless victim as the colonial authorities and the missionaries clashed over the form schooling should take -- literary education for religious indoctrination or preparation for semi-skilled jobs needed in the emerging Western-styled economy. Whether the missionaries were Christian or Islamic they were the primary educators in the early days of colonialism and they taught what they knew best--religious education.

As colonialism expanded, so did the semblance of a more structured system of education. For the most part the schools became more bookish with literary education dominating. This was the kind of education the Europeans found at home; it was the kind they were prepared to teach; it was the best they had to offer. There was little doubt that the Western-styled curriculum moved African students away from their cultural heritage. In the minds of the colonial leaders this is what they intended education to do. It was not long before African students saw colonial education as a means to move beyond their culture and the rural-oriented manual labor associated with it. A small minority took note of the semblance of Western society brought by the colonialists and opted to become a part of it no matter how it affected their indigenous way of life.

By the time political independence came to the continent there was a small group of Western educated Africans who became the new leaders of their nations. They saw in their schools an instrument to build a more cohesive society while moving their country forward. The challenge was to determine what to maintain, what to remove, and what to add to a formal educational system built by colonial rulers. The central question, for which there was not an easy answer, was -- in a school system that is elitist in its orientation, bookish and examination ridden, what is Western, what is modern and what is universal?

The Language Problem in the Schools

Nowhere is the dilemma of traditionalism versus modernism more evident than in the language policy found in educational systems throughout Africa. The policy, and the ensuing practice, remain an explosive issue in many countries today. While demands exist for a "national language," it is apparent that the ethnic tongues used in the nineteenth century are not sufficient to prepare the youth for the twenty-first century. Policies vary throughout the continent between the need to promote social and political cohesiveness through an African vernacular and the need for a European language to assist in the modernization process.

Some educators view the problem of language diversification as the most obvious barrier to progress on the continent. The multiplicity of traditional languages is viewed as an impairment to inter-African cooperation and the possibility of economic advancement through increased contact with multinational corporations throughout the world. These educators have recommended a language policy which would help establish an elite group with the ability to communicate effectively in the two main European languages found in Africa -- English and French.

Other educators are quick to reject the use of a foreign tongue in African schools. They stress the importance of the mother tongue to help safeguard their cultural heritage. An African tongue is seen as indispensable for understanding the richness of a tradition and for expanding the development of cultural expressions in many forms. Viewed from the perspective of national unity, an African tongue helps to develop a deeper appreciation of common linkages. These educators feel that a culture cannot endure very long separated from its language. With the majority of students never experiencing more than a basic education, exposure to a foreign language at an early age could help to remove children from the reality of their local environment, cause alienation between generations, and lead to the rejection of the African way of life.

For many countries one answer to the language dilemma has been a form of multilingual education. The extent of multilingualism on the continent makes it unique. It is not unusual for students to be exposed to their mother tongue, a regional vernacular and a European language while still in primary school. How to balance these languages in an educational system which must serve both rural and urban areas is still an open question. This is especially the case when fluency in a European language helps remove individuals from the harshness of rural life toward economic opportunity in the city. Yet nations need talented people to remain in the rural areas since agriculture is still the primary form of economic development.

Education For Self-Reliance or Technological Advancement

The need to balance rural realities with urban opportunities extends beyond language on the African continent. While the 1960's brought political independence to the continent, it was obvious that the economy was still closely tied to the former colonial power. Most nations of the world are dependent upon others for raw materials, markets, capital and technology. However, it was the extent of the dependence, and the narrow limits within it, which troubled the new leaders.

Most nations had inherited economics that were vulnerable to the demands of the Western world. Often economic development was tied to the export of a few raw materials, the import of Western finished products, and the lack of indigenous skilled people to help with the diversification of the economy. To alter this dependence was seen as an important step in decolonization. The manner in which this could be accomplished continues to be a subject of discussion, dispute and government policy.

One school of thought believes that development and economic growth can only come from inside their country; another school maintains that foreign aid, investment, and participation are essential in order to develop an economy which can compete on the world market. The government policy which emanates from these diverse opinions directly affects the educational system. Should the youth be schooled to produce a self-reliant economy based on the raw materials available or should they be educated to compete in a technologically advancing world; or is it possible to balance both while moving forward economically?

The East African nation of Tanzania is often seen as a country which pursued a policy of self-reliance and an educational system designed to support it. With independence the government developed a policy to bring about full participation of the people in the nation's economy while reducing dependency on the international market place. Toward this end the government called for establishment of larger communities where people would live and work together for the common good. The communities were to be organized around the principles of equality and cooperation, established on the basis of local conditions, and operate for the good of the country. Tanzania was to move from being a nation of individual peasant producers to a nation of large villages where the people would directly cooperate. The villages were identified as the main source of economic growth in rural areas and they were to provide their inhabitants with an opportunity to overcome social and economic inequalities.

The schools were expected to help in the movement toward self-reliant villages. The teachers in the village schools were expected to join their students in work and study, both in the classroom and in the agricultural fields. They also were asked to help their students develop proper attitudes toward cooperative work and to blur the distinction between manual labor and white collar work. The schools were to be the center of community activity and to provide a nationwide learning system designed to develop understanding and enthusiasm for the principle of self-reliance.

While Tanzania pursued a policy of self-reliance, several nations have attempted to modernize their economies and have turned to their educational systems to help. Nigeria was one example when it found itself with large oil reserves and an expanding modern economy. Kenya also has served as an example of a nation which attempted to balance efforts in agriculture and industrial development. Most recently, Ghana has attempted to establish policies which would encourage private incentives and the development of local and national industries.

These nations recognized the need to develop educational systems that would produce an educated labor force equipped to handle technological and industrial development. At times this meant an expansion of technical and vocational secondary schools. It also has meant the emergence of specialized postsecondary institutions to produce an educated cadre with specific managerial and technical skills. Often universities were enlisted to provide the kind of professional education which would promote a modern economy.

Whatever procedure was utilized to link education with modern economic development, nations are finding it difficult to balance educational qualifications with needed middle and high level person power. At times this is attributed to unrealistic employment objectives. However, in most cases national economies are not growing fast enough to accommodate the growing number of educated people. One result is large numbers of unemployed people in urban areas.

Whether nations pursue a policy of education for self-reliance, or for technological advancement, or a twin policy of both, difficult financial decisions must be made. Money for education is limited. What should the balance be between producing schools for everyone in order to help people meet basic needs and become self-reliant and supporting an educational system which will produce an elite corps of skilled personnel to further economic and modern development? The question is still under discussion.

Education for National Unity

To build a single nation out of a multiplicity of cultures is not an easy objective. The majority of political leaders on the continent face the challenge of moving their citizens away from local forms of social and political organizations, usually based on ethnicity, toward identity and allegiance to a modern nation. The schools are expected to be one major instrument in this process in several ways. The most obvious way is through what is taught in the schools. New books are being written and curriculum developed which give clear and positive information about the nation and its leaders. In addition to the formal curriculum, national songs are being sung, national pledges being made, and flags are being saluted. The goal is to shape the students' attitudes and values toward a national identity.

Teachers also are expected to assist in political socialization. Their training is often designed to help them better understand the political system and their role in promoting it. Their attitudes and interests become important in countering local influences and in inculcating a sense of obligation and loyalty to the nation. The goal of universal primary education, now found throughout the continent, is also associated with nation-building. With the majority of youth in the schools, a common network of communication can be established and a relationship developed between the government and the governed. Primary education also can produce literate citizens who can read government directed newspapers and reports.

Often the process of national integration is slow and difficult. While governments can exercise a strong influence in determining the purpose of education, students must identify with the purpose. At times there is a gap between what students and their parents expect from schooling and what the government wants. There can be a substantial difference between the teaching and learning of civic education for examination purposes and the actual following of the principles outside the classroom. In spite of these constraints, nation-building still remains one of the primary reasons why governments strongly support education. How the schools can best be utilized as an instrument for this purpose is still under discussion and debate.

Research on Education in Africa

Research on education in Africa can be divided into three historical periods. The first is the colonial and missionary period, the second the period which surrounds the independence movement during the 1960's, and the third is the decades of the 70's and 80's. This book focuses on the research which took place during the past two decades. However, a backdrop is necessary to help place the most recent research in perspective. This short introduction will attempt to do that by highlighting some of the most pertinent written works during the first two periods.

Colonial and Missionary Period

African societies have a rich history of educational tradition. All indigenous ethnic groups used education to transmit their cultural identity, develop appropriate skills for men and women, and prepare their youth to respond to the pressing problems found in their local communities. One of the first books published in the West that gave a detailed account of indigenous education was Jomo Kenyatta's *Facing Mt. Kenya* (Kenyatta, 1962). Kenyatta, Kenya's first president and one of the first Western educated anthropologists, initially published his book in 1938. In it he depicted traditional education as life itself with the goal of preparing youth for responsibilities as adults in a communal society. His book served as a guide for many Westerners who were attempting to understand traditional education.

The Western colonial period began with the Portuguese in

the fifteenth century and continues to this day. However, Western penetration into the continent did not begin in earnest until after the Berlin Conference of 1884 when the colonial powers divided Africa into spheres of influence. The early educators were missionaries who were encouraged by the work of David Livingstone. Two books in the English language which chronicled their early educational work were Roland Oliver's *The Missionary Factor in East Africa* (Oliver, 1952), and C. P. Groves' several volumes of *The Planting of Christianity in Africa* (Groves, 1955).

Following close behind the missionaries were the traders and colonial officials. The influence of missionary education on the life of the indigenous African became of great concern to them. The missionaries saw education as the road to evangelism and westernism, the colonial administrators and traders saw the need for trained help and skilled labor. To help clarify this situation and give direction to education two commissions went to Africa during the 1920's under the auspices of the Phelps-Stokes Fund in New York. Their reports remain landmark studies and are often the starting point for research on early attempts to Africanize the schools. Thomas Jesse Jones coordinated both reports: *Education in Africa* (Jones, 1922), and *Education in East Africa* (Jones, 1925). The main theme of both reports was that education should be adopted to the conditions and needs of African society.

This same theme was dominant in a series of reports which emanated from the British Colonial Office in London who saw the needs of the African as paramount, not the needs of the missionaries or the traders. The most prominent of these were *Educational Policy in British Topical Africa* (Great Britain, 1925), *Memorandum on the Education of African Communities* (Great Britain, 1935), and *Mass Education in African Society* (Great Britain, 1944).

By the end of World War II it was evident to the British Colonial Office that policy developed in London was not necessarily applied in the colonies. With this in mind, two study groups visited Africa in the early 50's and returned to write a definitive report which emphasized the need for educators to understand what the impact of the West had done to Africans. The report urged that educators prepare Africans to live in their own country. This could best be accomplished through a more liberal education based on the African environment and their own way of life. The report was entitled *African Education, a Study of Educational Policy and Practice in British Topical Africa* (Colonial Office and Nuffield Foundation, 1953).

Besides government documents, there were a few other

publications in the English language during this period that examined developments in African education. Most were written by colonial or missionary educators. Albert V. Murray's *The School in the Bush* described his tour of the schools throughout most of British colonial Africa (Murray, 1929), while Harold Jowitt's book *Suggested Methods for the African Schools* detailed methods for teaching Africans (Jowitt, 1934). The early work of Christian missionary educators was reviewed by B. D. Gibson in *The Remaking of Man in Africa* (Oldham & Gibson, 1931).

The Independence Movement

The decade of the 1960's brought independence to many African countries and with it a plethora of books and reports which attempted to chronicle the fast pace of educational expansion and to give some suggestions and guidance to its development. Bridging the independence movement were a few British authors. The best known were W. E. F. Ward, a colonial educator and prolific writer, who supplemented his articles in *The Colonial Review* with *Educating Young Nations* (Ward, 1959), Margaret Read, author of *Africans and Their Schools* (Read, 1953), and *Education and Social Change in Tropical Areas* (Read, 1955), and Leonard J. Lewis' *Educational Policy and Practice in British Tropical Areas* (Lewis, 1954), and *Education and Political Independence in Africa* (Lewis, 1962). Other writers from Great Britain who reviewed the educational scene in the 1960's included T. R. Batten in *Problems of African Development* (Batten, 1960), Adams Curle in *Educational Strategy for Developing Societies* (Curle, 1963), Guy Hunter's *Education for a Developing Region: A Study in East Africa* (Hunter, 1963), and Richard Jolly's *Education in Africa: Research and Action* (Jolly, 1969).

North Americans became increasingly interested in African education during the independence movement. Their activity was encouraged as newly emerging African nations were looking beyond their colonial past for educational ideas. Though limited in experience, they were productive in ideas. One organization early on the African scene was the Ruth Sloan Associates who produced a newsletter on African issues and commissioned individuals to survey the educational scene in the 1950's. Early in the 1960's, Helen Kitchen, under the auspices of the Ruth Sloan Associates, undertook a country by country survey of educational development in Africa. The book, *The Educated African* (Kitchen, 1962) became a standard reference source for Americans in the 1960's.

The Educated African was followed by several research studies, many of which were undertaken by individuals associated with

Teachers College, Columbia University. They included John Wilson's *Education and Changing West African Culture* (Wilson, 1963), David Scanlon's edited volumes of *Traditions of African Education* (Scanlon, 1964), and *Church, State and Education in Africa* (Scanlon, 1966) as well as Gray Cowan and others in *Education and National Building in Africa* (Cowan, O'Connell, Scanlon, 1965). During this period, several researchers noted the fast pace of educational expansion and the lack of data to give it direction. Those who attempted to make a contribution to the data base by assessing the relationship between education and the social and economic concerns of the society were Philip Foster in *Education and Social Change in Ghana* (Foster, 1965), Remi Clignet and Philip Foster in *The Fortunate Few: A Study of Secondary Schools and Students in the Ivory Coast* (Clignet & Foster, 1966), and George Urch in *The Africanization of the Curriculum in Kenya* (Urch, 1968).

The 1960's also saw the emergence of many African researchers and writers. The basic theme of their books tended to be on the need to move away from the colonial education pattern toward a system based on the uniqueness of African society. Among the most prominent authors were Kwame Nkrumah, the president of Ghana, who wrote *Africa Must Unite* (Nkrumah, 1963) and Julius K. Nyerere, the visionary leader of Tanzania, who wrote *Freedom and Socialism* (Nyerere, 1968). Two other prominent authors of this time were Kofi A. Busia, one time Prime Minister of Ghana who wrote *Purposeful Education for Africa* (Busia, 1964), and Abdou Moumini's *Education in Africa* (Moumini, 1968). In some ways they were the pioneers for a growing number of African researchers in the 1970's and 80's.

Perhaps the most important documents published in the 1960's were a series of UNESCO reports and publications that emanated from conferences designed to help the newly emerging nations plan and finance their educational development. The UNESCO publications, in turn, led to a series of individual national development plans. The most pertinent UNESCO document began with the Addis Ababa Conference in 1961, which developed an inventory of needs and priorities for African education, and established short- and long-term targets for the period 1960-80 (UNESCO, 1962a). Also meeting in Paris in 1962 were African educators, who attempted to adapt the general secondary school curricula to the African situation (UNESCO, 1962b). This was succeeded by the Tananarive Conference on the development of higher education on the continent (UNESCO, 1963). Two other conferences were held to determine the progress in meeting educational targets (UNESCO, 1968a) and to determine the trends in the financing of education (UNESCO, 1968b).

To move beyond the conference stage, UNESCO's International Institute for Educational Planning (IIEP) embarked in 1965 on a series of African case studies that attempted to highlight several major problems facing educational planners. The problems involved the relationship of education to economic development, the financing of education, teacher demand, adult education and the quality of education. Two senior staff members directed the studies in three English-speaking countries -- Nigeria, Tanzania and Uganda -- and two French-speaking countries -- the Ivory Coast and Senegal. They helped to produce a series of *African Research Monographs* published by UNESCO's IIEP in Paris during the late 1960's.

The 1970's and 80's

The past two decades saw a tremendous increase in the amount of research generated on the African continent. There were several reasons for this. The capability of African universities increased and special research centers began to emerge. In North America and Western Europe, a large number of African studies programs developed, some through government funds, others through individual and group initiative. Most of these programs had a strong research orientation. In addition to these developments, an increased number of Africans were seeking higher education in the West and East. Many of these students participated in research studies and took their skills back home with them.

During the 1970's and 80's, the educational problems faced by the newly emerging countries also became clearer. The rapid transition from colonial status to independence to participation on the international scene meant a shift in the kind of research that was needed. The early days of independence saw a dramatic increase in the number of students enrolled in all levels of schooling. The challenge to new governments in the 1960's focused on issues of rapid expansion and equality of opportunity. By the end of the 60's, the shift had begun toward a closer look at what a large financial investment in formal education could accomplish. The need to move away from the educational system inherited from the former colonial government also became clearer. Attempts to have the schools relate to their African heritage and contemporary social issues became a necessity. So did the need for governments to pursue the relationship between education and the need to build a national identity out of ethnic loyalty. The relations between economic development and skilled person power also had to be explored.

The 1980's saw governments begin to realize there were limits to the amount of money available to expand education. Enrollments began to stagnate, large numbers of students were dropping out or, through examinations, forced out of formal education and the overall quality of education became suspect. Increased investment without careful planning was risky; to support the planning more detailed research studies were necessary.

The kind of research studies that grew out of these issues are evident in the annotated bibliography. There was a movement away from general philosophical writing toward in-depth studies of specific problems identified in specific regions. There also were more international and regional conferences held where the focus was on a particular topic or challenge. Often these conferences were sponsored by international organizations such as UNESCO and the World Bank. Western governments also began to target more financial aid for particular educational concerns. Often part of the money was for research into the area under development. A good example of this can be found in the book's appendix where there is a list of some of the studies undertaken by the African Curriculum Organization which received financial assistance from the German Foundation for International Development.

One of the most dramatic shifts in the past two decades is most evident in this volume. It is the shift away from research studies dominated solely by Europeans and North Americans toward those conducted by Africans. The pace of progress in this area has been enhanced in several ways. There was more opportunity for graduate study where research was an integral part of the academic program. Also, more North American and European professional associations and societies were actively seeking African scholars to report their research findings at regional and national conferences. In addition, many African universities had developed to the point where research activities were encouraged and rewarded.

The 1970's and 80's have presented an exciting challenge to researchers on and away from the African continent. The results of their activities are evident in this publication which represents a good cross-section of people and topics that have been most visible in the world of research on African education.

BIBLIOGRAPHY

Batten, T.R. *Problems of African Development.* London: Oxford University Press, 1960.

Busia, Kofi A. *Purposeful Education for Africa*. London: Oxford University Press, 1964.

Clignet, Remi, and Philip Foster. *The Fortunate Few: A Study of Secondary Schools and Students in the Ivory Coast*. Evanston: Northwestern University Press, 1966.

Colonial Office and Nuffield Foundation. *African Education, A Study of Educational Policy and Practice in British Tropical Africa*. London: Oxford University Press, 1953.

Cowan, L. Gray, James O'Connell, and David G. Scanlon, eds. *Education and Nation-building in Africa*. New York: Frederick A. Praeger, 1965.

Curle, Adam. *Educational Strategy for Developing Societies*. London: Tavistock Publications Ltd., 1963.

Foster, Philip. *Education and Social Change in Ghana*. Chicago: University of Chicago Press, 1965.

Great Britain, Colonial Office, Advisory Committee on Native Education in the British Topical African Dependencies. *Educational Policy in British Topical Africa*. London: H.M.S.O., 1925.

Great Britain, Colonial Office, Advisory Committee on Education in the Colonies. *Memorandum on the Education of African Communities*. London: H.M.S.O., 1935.

_____. *Mass Education in African Society*. London: H.M.S.O., 1944.

Groves, C.P. *The Planting of Christianity in Africa* (Vol. 3). London: Lutterworth Press, 1955.

Hunter, Guy. *Education for a Developing Region. A Study in East Africa*. London: George Allen and Unwin Ltd., 1963.

Jolly, Richard, ed. *Education in Africa: Research and Action*. Nairobi: East African Publishing House, 1969.

Jones, Thomas Jesse. *Education in Africa*. New York: Phelps-Stokes Fund, 1925.

Phelps-Stokes Fund, 1922.

Jowitt, Harold. *Suggested Methods for the African Schools*. London: Longmans, Green and Co., 1934.

Kenyatta, Jomo. *Facing Mt. Kenya*. New York: Vantage Books, 1962.

Kitchen, Helen, ed. *The Educated African*. New York: Frederick A. Praeger, Inc., 1962.

Lewis, Leonard J. *Educational Policy and Practice in British Tropical Areas*. London: Thomas Nelson and Sons, Ltd., 1954.

Lewis, Leonard J. *Education and Political Independence in Africa*. Edinburgh: Thomas Nelson and Sons Ltd., 1962.

Moumini, Abdou. *Education in Africa*. New York: Frederick A. Praeger, 1968.

Murray, Albert V. *The School in the Bush*. London: Longmans, Green and Co., 1929.

Nkruman, Kwame. *Africa Must Unite*. New York: International Publishing Co., 1963.

Nyerere, Julius K. *Freedom and Socialism*. London: Oxford University Press, 1968.

Oldham, Joseph, and B.D. Gibson. *The Remaking of Man in Africa*. London: Oxford University Press, 1931.

Oliver, Roland. *The Missionary Factor in East Africa*. London: Longmans, Green and Co. Ltd., 1952.

Read, Margaret. *Africans and Their Schools*. London: Longmans, Green and Co. Ltd., 1953.

Read, Margaret. *Education and Social Change in Tropical Areas*. London: Thomas Nelson and Sons Ltd., 1955.

Scanlon, David G., ed. *Traditions of African Education*. New York: Teachers College, Columbia University Press, 1964.

Scanlon, David G., ed. *Church, State and Education in Africa*. New York: Teachers College, Columbia University Press,

1966.

UNESCO. *Final Report. Conference of African States on the Development of Education in Africa.* Addis Ababa: UNESCO, 1961.

UNESCO. *Final Report. Conference of Ministers of African Countries Participating in the Implementation of the Addis Ababa Plan.* Paris: UNESCO, 1962.

UNESCO. *Final Report of the Meeting of Experts on the Adaptation of the General Secondary School Curriculum in Africa.* Paris: UNESCO, 1962.

UNESCO. *The Development of Higher Education in Africa.* Paris: UNESCO, 1963.

UNESCO. *Regional Educational Targets and Achievements, 1960-65.* Paris: UNESCO, 1968.

UNESCO. *Trends in the Financing of Education in Certain African Countries.* Paris: UNESCO, 1968.

Urch, George E.F. *The Africanization of the Curriculum in Kenya.* Ann Arbor: Malloy Lithoprinting, Inc., 1968.

Ward, W.E.F. *Educating Young Nations.* London: George Allen and Unwin Ltd., 1959.

Wilson, John. *Education and Changing West African Culture.* New York: Teachers College, Columbia University Press, 1963.

End Notes

1. Fafunwa, A. Babs, and J.U. Aisiku, eds. *Education in Africa: A Comparative Survey.* London: George Allen and Unwin Ltd., 1982.
2. Nyerere, Julius, K. *The Arusha Declaration and TANU's Policy on Socialism and Self-Reliance.* Dar Es Salaam: Publicity Section, TANU, 1967.

AFRICA, GENERAL

History and Philosophy

Books

1.   Battle, Vincent M., and Charles H. Lyons, eds. *Essays in the History of Education*. New York: Teachers College Press, 1970.

Contains a series of essays drawn from M.A. theses and seminar papers submitted to the Center for Education in Africa, Teachers College, Columbia University. They represent the historical research conducted by graduate students affiliated with the Center. Topics range from early British thought and action in Africa to the initial years of the Jeanes School in Kenya. The book is one of a series on African education published by the Center.

2.   Datta, Ansu. *Education and Society: A Sociology of African Education*. London: Macmillan Publishers, 1984.

A study of the social bases of education in Anglophone Africa. The author uses a structural-functional approach to review six topics. He first discusses the way education is organized in different societies, and then analyzes the contribution education makes to those societies. The process by which children become members of a society also is described. The final section emphasizes the teacher's role in schools, an analysis of the classroom environment, and a review of the social factors that contribute to educational inequality in Africa.

3.   Harber, Clive. *Politics in African Education*. London: Macmillan Publishers Ltd., 1989.

Focuses on politics in primary and secondary schools and on the political knowledge and values of the students attending them. Some attention is paid to youngsters not in school. The book primarily is composed of case studies of selected countries. Among the themes and issues discussed are: the role of schools in nation-building; colonial education as a form of political domination; the role of political education in liberation struggles; the nature of political education courses in schools; and the need to consider the political views of young people.

4.   Manuwuike, Emeka. *Dysfunctionalism in African Education*. New York: Vantage Press, 1978.

An introduction to the philosophy of modern European education in Africa. The central thesis of the first section deals with Africa's search for identity as the educated become alienated from their heritage. The next section discusses the changes that occur when European academic subjects are superimposed on traditional education. A review of pertinent literature is an integral part of the book.

5.   Turner, Victor, ed. *Colonialism in Africa, 1870-1960. Vol. 3: Profiles of Change: African Society and Colonial Rule.* Cambridge: Cambridge University Press, 1971.

6.   Uchendu, Victor C., ed. *Education and Politics in Tropical Africa.* Buffalo: Conch Magazine Ltd., 1979.

The book grows out of a 1975 interdisciplinary seminar sponsored by the University of Illinois Africa Studies Program. Most chapters contain the papers given by participants and a formal paper by a discussant. The chapters appear in three sections entitled, The Political Content of Education, Unemployment, and Ethnicity; Education, Politicization, and National Development; and the Politics of Educational Change. Most chapters are by prominent academicians and are thought provoking.

Articles

7.   Adams, Milton N., and Medjama Coulibaly.   "Africa Traditional Pedagogy in a Modern Perspective." *Prospect* 15, No. 2 (1985): 275-80.

8.   Ball, Stephen J. "Imperialism, Social Control and the Colonial Curriculum in Africa." *Journal of Curriculum Studies* 15, No. 3 (1983): 237-83.

Examines the history of colonial education. Focuses on the confrontation between the demands of the indigenous people and the colonial government as well as conflicts between the different groups within the colonial system. The political purpose of education under colonialism is also explored.

9.   Boateng, Felix. "Africa Traditional Education: A Method of Disseminating Cultural Values." *Journal of Black Studies* 13, No. 3 (1983): 321-36.

Discusses how the philosophical foundations of traditional education served as a vehicle for communication between generations.

Comments on oral literature, secret societies and religious practices. Warns contemporary educators that a rejection of the past will create a loss of identity.

10. Marah, John Karefah. "Educational Adaptation and Pan Africanism: Trends in Africa." *Journal of Black Studies* 17, No. 4 (1987): 460-81.

Describes how colonial educators stressed African traditional values, and those values associated with being a dedicated worker, in an attempt to maintain power. In contrast the African nationalists of the 1960's rejected colonial education as an instrument of domination, and set the stage for the institutionalization of Pan-African education.

11. Nodoka, Otoni. "Moral Education in the Changing Traditional Societies of Sub-Saharan Africa." *International Review of Education* 26, No. 2 (1980): 153-70.

12. Ocaya-Lakidi, Dent. "Towards an African Philosophy of Education." *Prospects* 10, No. 1 (1980): 13-25.

13. Yoloye, E. Ayotunde."Dependence and Interdependence in Education: Two Case Studies from Africa." *Prospects* 15, No. 2 (1985): 239-50.

The three phenomena of independence, dependence and interdependence are examined through case studies of two regional African education organizations: the Science Education Programme for Africa and the African Curriculum Organization.

Education and Development

Books

14. Bellew, Rosemary. *African Education and Socio-Economic Indicators: An Annex to "Education Policies in Sub-Saharan Africa"*. Washington, D.C.: International Bank for Reconstruction and Development, 1986.

This World Bank publication contains statistical information on education along with related economic and social statistics. It provides information on the principal features of education for 39 countries in Sub-Saharan Africa. Excluded are Namibia and South Africa. The statistical information was supplied by UNESCO and supplemented with information from World Bank files and country documentations. A useful document for researchers and educational development specialists.

15.   Bray, Mark, Peter Clarke, and David Stephens. *Education and Society in Africa*. London: Edward Arnold Publishers Ltd., 1986.

Explores the relationship between education and the development of African societies through interaction at the international, national and community levels. Considers indigenous and Western-styled education with attention given to Islamic education.   Utilizes a comparative approach and detailed case studies to examine particular issues such as education and employment, education and social stratification, education and the community.

16.   Brown, Godfrey N., and Mervyn Hiskett, eds. *Conflict and Harmony in Education in Tropical Africa*. London: George Allen and Unwin Ltd., 1975.

Contains articles primarily written by British scholars.   The authors examine the underlying historical and cultural background in which educational planning and development can take place. Major sections are devoted to indigenous African education, Islamic education and the current situation.   The chapters range widely across tropical Africa and across the social science disciplines.   The book results from papers presented at a conference held in 1973 at the School of Oriental and African Studies, University of London.

17.   Fafunwa, A. Babs, and J.U. Aisiku, eds. *Education in Africa: A Comparative Survey*. London: George Allen and Unwin Ltd., 1982.

Offers a view of educational development from an African perspective.   Chapters are written on selected countries by leading African educators and tend to focus on the contemporary scene. Includes statistical information.   The introductory chapter discusses indigenous and Islamic education.

18.   Hawes, Hugh, and Trevor Coombe, eds. *Educational Priorities and Aid Responses in Sub-Saharan Africa*. London: HMSO Books, 1986.

The report of a 1984 conference held in Windsor, England and organized primarily by the University of London Institute of Education.   The conference brought together a cross-section of decision makers from Africa, senior officials from aid agencies and a few academics. Two background documents were prepared for the participants and are included in the book. One of the documents analyzes and reflects on the policies of selected aid agencies, the other contains an annotated bibliography of documents on aid to education in Africa. Also included are a synthesis of transcripts of commentary, lead papers from theme speakers and reports from working groups. The two major themes of the conference were priorities and aid.

19. International Labour Office. *Education for Development.* Geneva: International Labour Office, 1977.

A report from the fifth African Regional Conference held in Abidjan in 1977. The main emphasis is on how education, in all its forms, can facilitate the effective participation of individuals and groups in development efforts. Some attention is paid to what participation means. Areas of special emphasis include youth and the informal sector, the training of women, vocational and workers' education.

20. Makulu, H.F. *Education, Development and Nation-Building in Independent Africa.* London: SCM Press Ltd., 1971.

The author has written a series of essays which attempt to analyze such general topics as missionary and colonial education. He also interprets the role educators can play in the process of nation building as identified in educational conferences, reports and studies. The book is quite general, but does offer some good insights.

21. Mazrui, Ali A. *Political Values and the Educated Class in Africa.* Berkeley: University of California Press, 1978.

Represents the views and experiences of a well known "educated African and African educator." He views the book as a product of participant observation extending over many years. The chapters range widely and include essays on such subjects as, "A Study of Origins," "The Search for Relevance," and "Education, Dependency and Liberation." The opinions of the author, and the view of his experiences through his eyes, are worth reading.

22. Ponsionen, J.A., ed. *Educational Innovations in Africa: Politics and Administration.* The Hague: Institute of Social Studies, 1972.

Contains the papers and conclusions presented at a symposium on "Educational Innovations in Africa: Policies and Administration" held at Addis Ababa in 1971. The aim of the symposium was not to discuss the content of the innovation, but rather 'how to innovate' in order that the participants would think in terms of a process for planned change. The subject was restricted to sub-university levels of education. The chapters discuss examples in most of the African countries now members of the British Commonwealth.

23.   Thompson, A.R.   *Education and Development in Africa.* London: Macmillan Press Ltd., 1981.

An introduction to the role education can play in national development. Sections focus on social change, basic issues, how school systems are changing to meet national needs and current trends in educational reforms. Attention is paid to urban and rural development as well as to nonformal education. The book is intended for teachers in training and inservice and is one of a series of Macmillan International College editions designed for teacher education.

24.   UNESCO.   *Conference of Ministers of Education and Those Responsible for Economic Planning in African Member States.* Paris: UNESCO, 1982.

The final report of a UNESCO sponsored conference held in Harare, Zimbabwe in June-July of 1982. The conference was an attempt to help the participants link educational development with national economic plans.   A critique of the "Harare Conference" was undertaken by Samba Yacine Cisse in a 1986 UNESCO (Paris) publication.

25.   UNESCO.   *Education and Productive Work in Africa: A Regional Survey.* Dakar: UNESCO, 1982.

The survey was conducted by the Coordinating Unit of the Network of Educational Innovation for Development in Africa working out of the UNESCO Regional Office for Education in Africa, Dakar.

26.   UNESCO.   *Population-Education-Development: Africa South of the Sahara.* Dakar: UNESCO, 1971.

Reports on a UNESCO meeting of experts held in Dakar in 1971. The meeting studies the impact that education could have on population dynamics and the relationship between population dynamics and the economic, social and educational systems. The relationship was defined through documents prepared for the meeting as well as papers and discussion summaries given at the meeting. The meeting was called in order that UNESCO specialists would have a clearer idea of what research and activities they should sponsor relative to population education.

27. World Bank. *Education in Sub-Saharan Africa: Policies and Adjustment, Revitalization, and Expansion.* Washington, D.C.: World Bank, 1988.

A World Bank Policy Study that presents a framework within which countries may formulate strategies tailored to their own needs, and circumstances. It is designed to help identify common problems, provide leaders with comparative data and analytical tools, and suggest specific policy directions for consideration by national education authorities and donors. Sections are devoted to policy formation and options at all levels of formal education as well as an agenda for action. Highly recommended for those interested in the relationship between investment in education and national development.

Articles

28. Krieger, Milton. "African Policy Linking Education and Development: Standard Criticisms and a New Departure." *International Review of Education* 34, No. 3 (1988): 293-312.

29. McMahon, Walter. "The Relation of Education and R&D to Productivity Growth in the Developing Countries of Africa." *Economics of Education Review* 6, No. 2 (1987): 183-94.

Discusses the overall efficiency of investment in primary and secondary education. A high rate of return in investment was found by the author. Also explores technology transfer, capital investment and higher education development in relation to productivity growth.

30. Moock, Joyce Lewinger. "Overseas Training and National Development Objectives in Sub-Saharan Africa." *Comparative Education Review* 28, No. 2 (1984): 221-40.

Reviews the impact of overseas training on national development. Discusses the current economic crisis in Africa and the need for high-level, skilled workers. Considers the advantages and disadvantages of foreign study as a means of producing indigenous professionals. The article also notes the important research issues.

31. Mosha, Herme L. "The Role of African Universities in National Development: A Critical Analysis." *Comparative Education Review* 22, No. 2 (1986): 93-109.

Describes how economic and social problems hinder universities from participation in national development. Suggests ways for greater cooperation between government agencies and universities. Discusses the steps necessary to upgrade the curriculum.

32.   Omo-Fadaka,   Jimoh.   "Education   and   Endogenous Development in Africa." *Prospects* 12, No. 2 (1982): 261-68.

Suggests that development programs should focus on small-scale agriculture and industry, self-help villages and community based health programs in rural areas. Sees the need to develop educational programs appropriate for this type of rural development.

Primary

Books

33.   Bude, Udo.   *Primary Schools, Local Community and Development in Africa.*   Baden Baden: Nomos Verlagsgesellschaft, 1985.

A carefully researched analysis of the possible role primary education can play in local community development. The author reviews the need for relevance and reform in primary education to meet rising expectations of rural communities. A framework for the analysis is provided through an historical review of former reform efforts under colonial education. Comparisons are drawn between Western-styled education and that of selected African nations. A necessary volume for serious researchers interested in exploring the relationship between education and development.

Tertiary and Higher Education

Books

34.   Hanna, William John, ed. *University Students and African Politics*. New York: Africana Publishing Co., 1975.

Contains chapters written by the editor, and recognized Western scholars, that give detailed accounts and interpretations of university life in a series of African countries. The topics discussed range from students as an elite group, to their perception of the political situation in their own country, to their active involvement in politics. The book is the final in a series of studies of African students begun in 1963 under the general editorship of Seymour Martin Lipset.

35. Hinchliffe, Keith. *Higher Education in Sub-Saharan Africa*. London: Croom Helm, 1987.

Builds on the author's earlier work as a consultant for the World Bank. Attempts to bring together a wide range of materials which focus on the present and short term future of the labor market facing university graduates. Relates the financing of higher education to an economic return for the countries involved. The book contains a great deal of data on such topics as the higher education unit cost by country and within countries, by subject areas. An excellent critique of the possible economic influence on higher education.

36. Hinchliffe, Keith. *Issues Related to Higher Education in Sub-Saharan Africa*. Washington, D.C.: The World Bank, 1985.

Examines the growth and structure, the amount of resources used and the original rationale for the development of higher education on the continent. In addition, this "working document" analyzes the labor markets faced by graduates using a variety of data including rates of return, wage structures and trends, recorded vacancies, levels of expected employment and government policies. From the data, labor market assessments are constructed for 15 countries. The author is a lecturer in economics at the School of Development Studies, University of East Anglia.

37. Poth, Joseph. *National Languages and Teacher Training in Africa: A Methodological Guide for the Use of Teacher Training Institutes*. Paris: UNESCO, 1980.

38. Taylor, Andrew, ed. *Insights into African Education*. New York: Teachers College Press, 1984.

The book contains the Karl W. Bigelow memorial lectures including a tribute to the man. The lectures focus on higher education and teacher education. The primary authors are respected names in African education. Their essays are well written, insightful and lively.

39. Wandira, Asavia. *The African University in Development*. Johannesburg: Ravan Press, 1977.

A series of four essays which draw upon the experience of the author and his involvement in the academic and administrative work of Makerere University, Uganda, and the University College of Swaziland. The essays discuss the search for models which can guide university development, the special problems and opportunities of the "one country-one university" institution and the implications of university involvement in the development of out-of-school education.

40.   Yesufu, T.M., ed. *Creating the African University*. Ibadan: Oxford University Press, 1973.

Report on the proceedings of a workshop of the Association of African Universities held in Ghana in 1972. The workshop theme was "emerging issues of the 1970s." The five main themes under discussion were priorities, program development, staff development, research and continuing education. The heart of the book contains chapters which discuss 17 universities from the vantage point of the main themes.

Articles

41.   Eisemon, Thomas Owen, and Wilhelmus D. VanBalkom. "Universities and the Development of Scientific Capacity in African Countries: A Critique." *Compare* 18, No. 2 (1988): 105-16.

42.   McDowell, George R., and David, Wilcock. "Defining Equity and Excellence in Higher Education: Applying the American Land-Grant Model to African Agricultural Colleges." *Equity and Excellence* 22, No. 2-4 (1986); 52-57.

Applies specific definitions of equity and excellence to the nature of contemporary African agricultural problems, and   discusses the implication of these definitions for African institutions.

43.   Pelig, Margaret. "Leadership of Anglophone Tropical African Universities, 1948-1986." *International Journal of Educational Development* 6, No. 4 (1986): 245-62.

44.   Rathgeber, Eva M. "A Tenuous Relationship: The African University and Development Policymaking in the 1980's." *Higher Education* 17, No. 4 (1988): 397-410.

45.   Wandira, Asavia.   "University and Community Evolving Perceptions of the African University." *Higher Education* 10, No. 3 (1981): 253-73.

46.   Young, M.Crawford. "The African University: Universalism, Development and Ethnicity." *Comparative Education Review* 25, No. 2 (1981): 145-63.

Specialized Education   (Adult, Community, Nonformal, Technical, Vocational)

Books

47.   Kabwaga,   Antoine,   and   Martin   M.   Kaunda,   eds.
Correspondence Education in Africa. London: Routledge and
Kegan Paul, 1973.

A series of case studies that describe examples of correspondence
education on the continent. The studies include such subjects as rural
education, professional and administrative training, teacher training
and the UN correspondence training program. One section contains
a survey of African correspondence institutions.

48.   King, Kenneth, ed.   *Education and Community in Africa*.
Edinburgh: Centre   of   African   Studies,   University   of
Edinburgh, 1976.

Proceedings of a seminar held in the Centre of African Studies,
University of Edinburgh in 1976. The introductory chapters discuss
the role and practices of community education in Africa. The
chapters which follow are a series of case studies that describe
education and community development activities in various
Anglophone African countries.

49.   McNown, John S., ed. *Technical Education in Africa*. Nairobi:
East Africa Publishing House, 1970.

The book primarily relates to a conference on engineering education
held in Ghana in 1967. The conference was designed to help
strengthen the education of engineers in universities and technical
institutes.   The background papers emphasize the system that
presently was being used to produce engineers and technicians.
Papers associated with the conference focus on how technical
education should be organized and the present weaknesses and
strengths.   There also is a list of various facilities for technical
education and a comparative analysis of the use being made of them.

50.   Richmond, Edmun B. *A Comparative Survey of Seven Adult
Functional Literacy Programs in Sub-Saharan Africa*. Lanham:
University Press of America, Inc., 1986.

The seven programs surveyed are found throughout the continent.
The author also includes a longitudinal examination of Adult
Functional Literacy in Mali from 1959-1988.   The introductory

chapter develops a strong rationale for functional literacy programs. The book contains illustrations and helpful figures.

51.   Wood, A.W. *Informal Education and Development in Africa.* The Hague: Mouton, 1974.

A publication of the Institute of Social Studies, the Hague, which attempts to assess the reasons why out-of-school opportunities have expanded so rapidly in recent years. The study carefully critiques the evolution of out-of-school and training programs for primary school learners in the twelve Commonwealth countries. Methodologies are compared and conclusions drawn.

Articles

52.   Alaezi, O. "A Critique of the Vocalization of the African Curriculum." *Vocational Aspect of Education* 37, No. 97 (1985); 57-60.

An analysis of attempts made to vocationalize the school curriculum. Links school work with knowledge of the local community in order to equip students with skills for self-help efforts as well as for the modern economy. Teachers are expected to work along side their students and utilize local materials.

53.   King, Kenneth. "The New Politics of Job Training and Work Training in Africa." *International Journal of Educational Development* 8, No. 3 (1980): 153-62.

54.   Urevbu, Andrew O. "Vocationalizing the Secondary School Curriculum: The African Experience." *International Review of Education* 34, No. 2 (1988): 258-69.

Curriculum and Methods

Books

55.   Awoniyi, Timothy Adedji. *The Teaching of African Languages.* London: Hodder and Stoughton, 1982.

56.   Bude, Udo, ed. *Curriculum Development in Africa.* Bonn: German Foundation for International Development, 1983.

Summarizes and highlights the most important trends in curriculum development discussed at a 1982 conference held in Swaziland and attended by participants from 16 'African Curriculum Organization' member countries. The national curriculum institutions participating in the conference prepared "state of the art" reports which are an important part of the book. Also included are extracts from an evaluation report on past and future curricular activities that was distributed in advance to participants. The report was prepared by Professor E. A. Yoloye, Chair of the African Curriculum Organization, and served as a reference point for discussions.

57. Davies, Alan, ed. *Language in Education in Africa*. Edinburgh: Centre of African Studies, University of Edinburgh, 1986.

The proceedings of a 1985 seminar held at the University of Edinburgh. The content is a series of case studies on language policy, planning and use in selected countries. Topics include patterns of language use, attitudes toward the use of English, multilingualism and an agenda for research in the next decade. The case studies range from the very general coverage of a topic to the specific. There is also a wide range in the quality of the research.

58. Erny, Pierre. *The Child and His Environment in Black Africa: An Essay on Traditional Education*. Nairobi: Oxford University Press, 1981.

Contains a series of studies on the life of African children in their traditional environment and the role of education in that environment. The French author primarily focuses on educational practice and pedagogy. He is aware that African educators are searching for ways to integrate the 'best' of traditional education into the contemporary curriculum. The book is very detailed and highly informative.

59. Hawes, Hugh, ed. *Curriculum and Reality in African Primary Schools*. London: Longman Group Ltd., 1979.

A detailed and practical book with four authors cooperating on the content. The focus is on English-speaking Africa with specific examples of how curriculum time is allocated in ten countries. Sections include strategies for planning, the content of the curriculum and proposals for implementation. In writing the book, the authors drew upon their own experience, collected materials from ten countries, and interviewed professionals in curriculum development centers, universities and ministries in Africa. A good investment for curriculum planners and implementors.

60. Nandwa, Jane, and Austin Bukenya. *African Oral Literature*

for Schools. Nairobi: Longman Kenya, 1983.

61.   UNESCO. *Handbook for Biology Teachers in Africa*. Paris: UNESCO, 1986.

Articles

62.   Ajayi-Dopemu, Yinka. "Visual Aids and the Enhancement of Communication in Africa." *Journal of Educational Television* 8, No. 3 (1982): 203-209.

Discusses the differences in perception and interpretation of visual aids between African and Western students in general terms. Suggests that the implications of these differences be considered in producing learning materials.

63.   Bajah, Sam Tunde. "Primary Science Curriculum Development in Africa: Strategies, Problems and Prospects with Particular Reference to the African Primary Science Programme." *European Journal of Science Education* 3, No. 3 (1981): 259-269.

The African Primary Science Programme was a major project undertaken by the Educational Development Center, Newton, MA. The problems and implications of introducing the program are discussed in this article.

64.   Barth, James. "The New Social Studies of the 70's Survives in Africa in the 80's" *The Social Studies Teacher* 8, No. 1 (1986): 9.

65.   Crane, Louise. "African Arts and the Social Studies." *Social Education* 46, No. 7 (1982): 502-07.

Suggests specific ways in which African literature, sculpture, music, dance and theater can be made more available to the social studies curriculum in the primary and secondary schools.   Includes a bibliography of print and nonprint materials.

66.   Mba, Peter. "Trends in Education of Handicapped Children in Developing Countries with Particular Reference to Africa." *Journal of Special Education* 7, No. 3 (1983): 273-78.

Describes the results of a survey of special education needs. Indicates that only a small percentage of special needs children receive schooling and that opportunities for training special educators are scarce.

67.   Murphy, Catherine, and JoElla Walters.   "Design Training
      Problems in the Developing World: Experience in Africa."
      Performance and Instruction 21, No. 6 (1982): 26-29.

Explores four categories of information needed to develop realistic
training programs.   Describes a set of workshops on nursing in
conjunction with the Ministry of Health in an African country.
Considers the effectiveness of workshops on program development.

68.   Nichter, Richard. "International Science Education: A Study
      of UNESCO Science Education Improvement Projects in
      Selected Anglophone Countries of Africa." *Science Education*
      68, No. 4 (1984): 381-96.

Describes some of the problems, and the reasons for the problems,
faced by technical advisors attempting to implement projects designed
to improve science education.   Some of the problems discussed
include finances, underestimating the process, motivation and
personality conflicts.   A list of major UNESCO field projects is
included.

69.   Ogunniyi, M.B.   "Two Decades of Science Education in
      Africa." *Science Education* 70, No. 2 (1986):   111-22.

Analyzes the nature of science teaching and curriculum development;
suggests future directions. Includes a table which lists major African
curriculum projects.

70.   Perraton, Hilary. "Radio Broadcasting and Public Education
      in Africa." *Educational Media International* 4 (1981): 4-10.

Examines the use of radio for distance learning by focusing on the
upgrading of teachers. Eighteen references are listed.

Teachers

Books

71.   Bude, Udo, and Jeremy Greenland, eds. *Inservice Education
      and Training of Primary School Teachers in Anglophone Africa.*
      Baden Baden: Nomos Verlagsgesellschaft, 1983.

Contains the conference report on the Dissemination Conference of
Eastern, Central and Southern Africa held in Zimbabwe in 1982. The

report surveys inservice education and training for primary school teachers in thirteen countries. In addition to the survey, each country reported on one particular innovative strategy which could be replicated elsewhere.

72.   Hanson, John W., and D.J.S. Crozier, eds. *Report on the Supply of Secondary Level Teachers in English-Speaking Africa.* East Lansing: Michigan State University, 1974.

A comprehensive and analytical report which focuses on the problem of determining the likely demand for overseas personnel for staffing secondary level institutions. It is the last of sixteen individual country reports and as a consequence summarizes findings. The first section contains strategies for localization and the second describes major social, political and economic factors likely to affect educational development and teacher supply. The final section contains some excellent statistical, documentary and bibliographic resources. Very detailed, good use of statistical information.

73.   Poth, Joseph. *National Languages and Teacher Training in Africa: A Methodological Guide for the Use of Teacher Training Institutes.* Paris: UNESCO, 1980.

Religion and Private Education

Books

74.   Berman, Edward H., ed. *African Reactions to Missionary Education.* New York: Teachers College Press, 1975.

Presents the recollections of seven Africans who went through mission supported school systems in different parts of the continent. The book brings out the human side of the experience with vivid illustrations. In the opening and concluding chapters the author analyzes missionary education within the historical forces that shaped it and led to its decline. The author's introductory sections to each of the chapters is very helpful.

75.   Megill, Esther L. *Education in the African Church.* London: Chapman, 1980.

Article

76.   Nduka, Otonti. "Moral Education in the Changing Traditional Societies of Sub-Saharan Africa." *International Review of Education* 26, No. 2 (1980): 153-70.

Describes how traditional moral education is presented in schools as Christian instruction. Notes difficulties in integrating western and indigenous values and recommends more cooperation between schools, the home and society at large.

Education for Women

Articles

77.   Sudarkasa, Niara. "Sex Roles, Education and Development in Africa," *Anthropology and Education* 13, No. 2 (1982): 279-88.

Discusses changing patterns in educational and occupational sex roles in twentieth-century Africa by focusing on the changing position of women. Describes the effects of colonial rule.

WEST AFRICA

Since independence came to the countries of West Africa the most impressive educational feature has been the rapid rate of expansion. During the past thirty years the number of students enrolled at all levels has more than quadrupled. Country after country has introduced some form of universal or compulsory primary education, built more secondary schools and opened at least one national university. This massive expansion has been made possible through the infusion of large sums of money by new governments who saw the quick expansion of educational opportunity as a political necessity.

Often the challenge of expansion left little time to think about the relationship of education to national needs. Slowly the focus has shifted away from the numbers enrolled in the schools toward the management of education and the curriculm being taught in the classrooms. As national leaders take a closer look at both the structure and function of their educational systems they find that the two contemporary forces that still strongly influence the schools are the aftermath of colonialism and religion.

Formal education came early to West Africa and it was most often in the form of missionary education. In the northern and eastern sections of most West African countries the influence of Islam was considerable. Islamic schools could be found inside and outside of mosques and in specially built schools. The primary goals of these schools were to teach in Arabic the Koran, the holy book of the faith, and the guiding principles of the religion. The Christian missionaries' influence was strongest on the Atlantic coast and to some degree penetrated inland. Their conscious effort was to use the schools as transmitters of Christian moral values and as an instrument to help build attitudes toward Western cultural values, often to the detriment and neglect of indigenous values.

Except for Liberia all the countries of West Africa came under the influence of the British and French colonialists. Quite early Great Britain recognized the possibility of governing their colonies through "indirect rule" which was similar to the way they ruled India. "Indirect rule" called for colonial governors to rule with the assistance of local indigenous leaders. France, on the other hand, endeavored to bring its colonies within its political and cultural sphere. This meant the duplication of the French government and its civil service throughout its colonies. Deputies from these colonies were elected to the French National Assemblies in Paris.

The different colonial attitudes influenced education. As early as the 1920's schools in the French colonies were expected to conform to the quality, structure and curriculum of their counterpart in France. The general goal was to develop a small core of French-speaking indigenous citizens who would uphold the French way of life. Assimilation was the objective.

The British never had a firm control over their West African colonies. Their "indirect rule" policy encouraged diverse educational systems, organized primarily by church related voluntary agencies. Often these schools encouraged local languages and made some attempt to adapt their curriculum to the local environment. However, most British colonial teachers, and British trained African teachers, usually saw in English literary education the "best" in education. It was the only form of education they knew and therefore they taught it. One consequence was the wholesale borrowing of the British model with its structure and often with its curriculum and language.

With independence some West African nations made strong efforts to wrestle control of education away from religious and conservative colonial educators. Other nations were content to utilize the structure that existed and concentrate on the growing demand for more education. Whatever initial pattern was followed after independence, the challenge today is to relate education to national development goals.

The most common national goals found throughout West Africa can be placed in three categories. First is the need to build national unity. Most countries inherited the problems of a heterogeneous and linguistically diverse population bound together in a nation with boundaries drawn by the colonial powers. The challenge is to use the schools to build a sense of nationhood. The second goal is to revive the traditional values of African culture. By emphasizing what is good and respected in traditional culture the schools are being asked to build pride and promote social cohesiveness. West African countries have attempted to pay particular attention to traditional values. The third goal is to align the educational system with the need for economic development. This means an increased emphasis on producing the middle level trained personnel through more and improved technical and vocational education, and the development of highly trained personnel to manage the nation's economy. It also means providing more educational opportunity for women in order that their talents can be utilized.

In most of the West African nations there is a gap between what the government would like to accomplish through its schools and what is actually happening. To better understand that gap, and the contemporary educational scene, the following section highlights the distinctiveness of each major country and explores its educational structure and how that structure functions.

BENIN

Overview

Formerly referred to as Dahomey when it was a French colony, this country of five million people was one of the areas on the west coast that came into contact with Europeans quite early. One result was that prior to independence in 1960 close to half the school children were enrolled in Roman Catholic mission schools. French-modeled secondary education also was available for a few. The relatively large number of professionals and intellectuals caused the colony to be called Africa's Latin Quarter.

Since independence the government has assumed control of education and moved toward a decentralized administrative structure. The new leaders called upon local communities to contribute some of the work and money necessary to build local schools. A reform program in 1974 made education free, public, secular and compulsory. It also attempted to equalize the geographical distribution of educational opportunity. The implementation of these goals has met some difficulties including the lack of finances and adequately trained teachers. However, by 1980 over 60% of primary-aged children were enrolled in school.

Structure

The Ministry of Primary Education and the Ministry of Secondary and Higher Education administer the schools. The basic structure consists of a compulsory 6-year primary school, a 4-year junior secondary, and a 3-year senior secondary school. Attempts are being made to develop secondary technical and specialized schools, but 98% of all secondary students attend a general secondary school with a strong academic orientation. The University of Benin was founded in 1971 and remains the country's only university. Some efforts have been made to educate adults in the rural areas, but the literacy rate has been estimated at only 26%.

Function

Attempts are being made to adapt the curriculum to national needs and to locally produce textbooks and teaching materials. This is necessary in order to place greater emphasis on agriculture and technology in the schools. Unfortunately these attempts are hampered by a lack of trained staff. The medium of instruction at all levels is French and the overall system still retains a French manner. The university is making efforts to produce the skilled personnel needed by the country. To assist in this process an institute for training public administrators and another for regional development are now producing graduates.

BURKINA FASO

Overview

Formerly named Upper Volta, this semiarid nation was a French colony prior to independence in 1960. The lack of income generating exports makes it difficult for the government to devote large sums of money to formal education. Nevertheless, efforts have been made to extend educational opportunity to rural areas and to provide vocational education related to agricultural development. Much of the effort involves literacy campaigns. The country has one of the world's highest illiteracy rates. Recently the government has attempted to reduce the cost of teachers by restructuring the work force. Although the salaries are modest by international standards, they are very high in comparison with the country's income level and consume 98% of the primary education budget.

Structure

The Ministry of Education administers all but a few institutions. Within the Ministry, the Director General of National Education manages primary, secondary, agricultural, technical and teacher education. The Director of the Office of Higher Education serves as Rector of Ouagadougou University. Although primary education is compulsory for 6 years, less than 20% of the eligible children complete the full cycle. Primary education is followed by a 4-year junior secondary school and a 3-year senior secondary school. Technical education is provided in separate institutions while higher education is provided at Ouagadougou University and its affiliated institutions.

Function

The overall curriculum continues to be based on the French model. Efforts are being made to introduce indigenous languages, but for the most part French is the language of instruction at all levels. Slightly more than half the secondary schools are private and mainly church related. Young women make up only a small percentage of those in the secondary schools, but the number is increasing. Great strides are being made to promote rural and agricultural education through radio broadcasting and the development of over 800 rural centers that distribute information. In order to assist in this effort the government has developed an Institute of Agriculture that offers a five-year course after senior secondary school.

CÔTE D'IVOIRE

Overview

Soon after independence was attained from the French, the nation introduced a major educational reform that emphasized civic responsibility and basic literacy through an expanded primary school system. The reform also introduced scientific and technical education into the secondary and higher educational effort in order to produce a cadre of well qualified personnel. Again in 1976 the government introduced a new reform which placed education in a pivotal role in the country's five-year development plan. The result has been a dramatic expansion in the number of schools and students during the past ten years. The educational expansion, and a concomitant infrastructure to support it, has been made possible by sustained economic growth as a result of a close Eurafrican partnership. While the economy has stagnated in the past few years, the government's financial efforts to promote the expansion of education is among the most impressive on the continent.

Structure

Education is a centrally managed and controlled enterprise with supervision extending down to the local level. Most new programs are initiated through presidential decrees and orders from the four ministries -- Ministry of Primary Schools and Instructional Television, the Ministry of National Education, responsible for secondary and university education, The Ministry of Technical Education and Professional Training and the Ministry of Popular Education, Youth and Sports. The educational ladder is a replica of the French system with a 6-year primary school, followed by a 7 year secondary cycle. The latter is divided into a 4-year cycle, and topped by the final 3 years. The external examination system is closely allied to that of France and students must pass rigorous testing at the end of each cycle.

Function

The National Reform Commission in the mid-1970's attempted to move the curriculum away from the French model, but without much success. French is the language of instruction at all levels and is viewed as a unifying force in a nation with over 60 different languages. Knowledge of the nation's cultural values is emphasized at the primary level. The country pioneered the use of educational television at the primary level in an effort to reach rural areas, but the attempt proved too costly. The secondary schools are expected to maintain educational quality and produce the country's middle level manpower. Recent reform efforts are concentrating on the development of technical and vocational education. The National University of the Ivory Coast maintains a reputation for excellence. However, its effort to meet high level manpower needs falls short with the large majority of students enrolled in the humanities rather than in the scientific and technological fields.

The Ivory Coast is often used as an example of a nation that has attempted to relate education to social and economic needs. The reform movements are assisting in these efforts. However, the close adherence to the French ideal of a classic academic education is proving to be a hindrance.

GAMBIA

Overview

The nation has the distinction of being the smallest state in Africa. Its geographical boundaries extend only a short distance from the Gambia River. A former British colony surrounded by Francophone countries, its existence has depended upon the use of the river and its tributaries for trade. Education is influenced by its colonial heritage and a population that is approximately 80% Moslem. Prior to independence in 1965, Western schooling was dominated by missionary groups with the exception of the Koranic schools that functioned at the primary level. The nation faces a large illiteracy rate among its adult population, who have been more interested in trade and farming in the rich delta area than in formal education.

Structure

Education is under the control of the government today and is headed by the Ministry of Education, Youth and Sports. A 6-year primary school is free, but not compulsory. Those students who score well on the West African Examination Council test enter a 5-year secondary school. An additional examination, The General Certificate of Education, ordinary level, determines the few students who receive a place at one of the nation's two academic secondary schools. These schools offer an additional two-year course leading to the advanced level General Certificate of Education examination. Parallel to the academic secondary schools are both private and public vocational and technical schools. Gambia does not have a university, but there are post-secondary colleges that train teachers, nurses and agricultural specialists.

Function

The official language in the schools is English. Attempts are being made to indigenize the curriculum at the primary level, but a British academic pattern dominates the secondary schools. The government is concentrating on the expansion of primary education. However, a lack of teachers has slowed educational development as has the lack of education in rural areas. With 90% of the population engaged in agriculture the government has difficulty convincing some rural dwellers of the benefits of formal education.

GHANA

Overview

This former British colony has a long tradition in the development of formal Western-styled education. It was introduced first by Christian missionaries and then supported by the colonial government. The tradition stems from the early contact between Africans and Europeans along the coast, both for purposes of trade and proselytizing. Ghana was in the forefront of the independence movement on the continent and in 1957 an independent government announced that educational development was to be the key to the nation's progress. During the 1960's its expanding educational system produced graduates who were highly regarded and the country became an important recruiting arena for many countries and international organizations seeking civil servants and educators. Unfortunately a series of military coups and counter coups left an unstable government and a neglected educational system. The political stability of the past few years has encouraged new educational efforts and with a solid core of teachers and administrators the future could be bright.

Structure

Formal education is highly structured throughout the country. While the Ministry of Education and Culture is responsible for the overall management of the system, it is assisted by such organizations as the Ghana Education Service, the Institute of Professional Studies and the Council for Higher Education. The nine regions of the country are administered by a Director of Education, who is responsible for the inspection and supervision of schools in the region. Each region is further divided into districts where an Assistant Director of Education assumes responsibility for primary and middle schools. The attempt to decentralize has made the people in each district accountable for aiding their own schools. National policy has made ten years of education free and compulsory and has led to the establishment of secondary schools subsidized by the central government.

The educational ladder consists of 6 years of primary schooling followed by a 4-year middle school prior to secondary education. A new system introduced early in the 80's eliminated middle schools in favor of a 3-year junior secondary school, but much of the plan has not yet been implemented. To enter senior secondary school students must pass an external examination administered by the West African Examination Council. The 5-year secondary cycle is divided into 3 years of general education followed by specialized study leading to the advanced level external exam. Along the educational ladder those who do not pass the examinations have opportunities to enter teacher training colleges, technical schools, polytechnics and vocational training centers. Many of these schools have not been developed as much as the government would like to see. At the top of the education structure are three universities -- The University of Ghana founded in 1948, the University of Cape Coast and the University of Science and Technology.

Function

In the mid 1980's the curriculum was again modified and adapted to traditional cultural values. A Curriculum Enrichment Programme was given charge of implementing new goals in cultural education. The language of instruction during the first 3 primary years is the main Ghanian language of the area. After that English is the sole language of instruction. Ghana has a relatively large urban population and quite often schooling begins there in the English language. There are 12 secondary schools that enjoy a great deal of prestige because of historical precedents and the good academic performance of their students. These institutions have a curriculum that is academic and British in its orientation. Recently the number of technical institutions has been increased. Relatively large numbers of students seek higher education overseas.

GUINEA

Overview

Soon after independence the new president instituted a series of dramatic reforms designed to move the nation toward a socialist ideology. All schools were nationalized. Church-operated schools came under government direction and wherever possible the curriculum was Africanized. The teaching force also was Africanized and the French language was replaced with indigenous languages of instruction. A greater emphasis also was placed on practical subjects. Unfortunately many of the planned educational reforms were lost in a bureaucratic maze or were not implemented due to a lack of funds. Still, Guinea is often cited as a nation that moved quickly away from the colonial past and charted its own independent course.

Structure

Education is administered by a cabinet office called the Education and Culture Domain. Responsibility is divided between the Minister of Pre-University Education and Literacy and the Minister of Higher Education and Scientific Research. Below the national level are regional offices and a series of inspectors. Local communities are expected to help in the construction of primary schools, but for the most part, what funds are available flow from the central government. The primary education cycle lasts for 6 years and an estimated 80% of eligible children are in school. Compulsory education until age 14 and government-sponsored adult literacy courses are designed to raise the literacy rate beyond 30%. Both primary and secondary enrollment dramatically increased during the past two decades.

The secondary cycle consists of a first level of 4 years followed by an additional 3 years with state examinations determining who continues. The strong emphasis on vocational education resumes at the secondary level and an effort is made to link studies more closely to the practical needs of the local area. Higher education includes the University of Conakry, opened soon after independence, and the University of Kankan as well as advanced education in teacher training, agriculture and mining. The universities offer 5-year academic programs while the other institutions have courses that vary in length.

Function

The country's efforts to provide all children with a primary education and to train a cadre of skilled personnel to meet the nations' needs require most of the money available. At the primary level students are expected to contribute to community life through practical activities. Pressure to use French as the language of instruction at all levels is increasing. So is the effort to place more emphasis on academic secondary education to the detriment of advances made in technical and vocational education. It appears that Guinea is entering a new period of educational development where the movement is toward increased academic quality.

LIBERIA

Overview

Liberia often has been acknowledged as the continent's first independent state. The nation tends to trace its beginning to the settlement in the 1820's of North American Blacks who mingled with and politically dominated the ethnic groups residing in the area. An independent nation was declared in 1847 and for the next 100 years the formal education that did exist was primarily in the hands of Christian missionaries. In the 1950's the government began to take control and, assisted by foreign aid, enrollment in the schools grew quickly and at all levels. By the 1980's over 75% of the eligible school children were enrolled in primary schools and the secondary schools enrolled 23% of the relevant age cohort. Unfortunately the administrative structure did not keep pace with the rapid development of schools and the system often has been identified as one that is poorly managed with a high wastage rate and capable of absorbing foreign aid without noticeable results. What the future holds is difficult to say. The nation is emerging from a bloody and divisive civil war. The division is most often along ethnic lines. One major question is whether the semblance of national unity can be developed over time.

Structure

Continuing political unrest in the 1980's precluded attention being given to education. Even under peaceful conditions the centralized system only receives a small percentage of the nation's budget. However, the budget is often supplemented by missionary efforts, some private enterprise and a good deal of foreign aid, most often from the United States. The Ministry of Education controls the schools and utilizes country and local supervisors as its agents. Primary education is free, compulsory, 6 years in duration and similar to that in the United States. Only about 15% of those who enter elementary school complete it. The drop out rate also is very high at the secondary level which is divided into junior and senior high school, each 3 years in duration. Some advances are being made in the development of vocational and technical schools, but a lack of money hinders development. Unlike most of Sub-Saharan Africa, advancing from one level of education to the next does not depend on the results of an external examination. The University of Liberia also has a generous admissions policy. Admission is open to any high school graduate who can pass a required test in English and mathematics. Most students pass the test, but only one-third of those admitted receive degrees.

Operating parallel to the formal system is a traditional system that still functions in many rural areas. It usually takes place in a "bush" school developed by ethnic groups. The school lasts 3-4 years and requires students to remove themselves from society and live in a secluded area. Successful completion of the school is necessary in order to become an accepted member of the adult group.

Function

The National Curriculum Development Center of the Ministry of Education is responsible for the development of materials and the conducting of seminars and workshops for teachers. The Center established more than a dozen rural outposts where teacher workshops are held. The curriculum is patterned after that of the United States including the textbooks and classroom material. Overall the schools are characterized as lacking order and discipline with teachers that lack motivation. Whether a reformed system will emerge from the civil war is difficult to predict.

MALI

Overview

Soon after independence in 1960 the new government introduced reforms that were designed to move education away from the French colonial model. A popular slogan at the time was "rush to school" and the youth did. Unfortunately the demand for schooling far exceeded the limited resources available in this semi-arid, economically poor nation. Officially 9 years of schooling became compulsory, but the ability to supply enough schools became difficult, especially in rural areas. Another difficulty arose around language usage in the schools. The government attempted to promote indigenous languages instead of French. However the indigenous languages handicapped those who wanted to succeed in secondary education. One result is the evolution of a two-tiered system where the few who have had the opportunity to pursue French are now part of an elite group.

During recent years the Malian government has made great strides in promoting adult literacy campaigns to overcome the lack of opportunity for formal education. Unfortunately the illiteracy rate among adults is still one of the highest on the continent.

Structure

Mali has a centralized system of education with control below the ministry level vested in school inspectors located in each of the six regions in the country. Primary education is 9 years in duration with a 6-year cycle followed by 3 additional years. Entrance to the last 3 years is through an external examination, as is entrance to either an academic or technical secondary school. There is a recent trend to move away from boarding schools at the secondary level toward day schools in order to accommodate more students. There is no university in Mali, but there are a series of higher education centers that offer degree courses lasting from 2 to 7 years. They include a Higher Teacher Training College, the rural polytechnic institutes and schools for administration, medicine, and engineers.

Function

The first 6 years of primary education is divided into 2 years each of "initiation," "aptitude" and "orientation." The last 3 years is an extension of the first 6 years. Those who gain admission to an academic secondary grammar school have 2 years of general education followed by specialization in three subject areas within the field of literature, biological sciences and pure sciences. These schools prepare students for higher education. Technical schools are designed to prepare students for direct entrance into employment. They are available in such fields as agriculture, industry, commerce, administration and nursing.

MAURITANIA

Overview

This "Islamic Republic" of two million people bridges the Arab and African cultures in the northwest of the continent. The African minority, who primarily live along the Senegal River Valley, had the advantage of formal schooling during the French colonial period. One consequence was the emergence of an elite French speaking group among them. While political control today is vested in the Arab majority, most school facilities are located in the south along the Senegal River. Two-thirds of the rest of the country is primarily a desert of shifting sands where almost 70% of the nomadic population lives. The government faces some resistance toward formal education by the nomads. One result is a very low literacy rate among adults.

Structure

The Ministry of National Education directs the educational system as well as the nation's Islamization program. In an attempt to unify the country under the Islamic religion the traditional Koranic schools are integrated into the public system. The educational structure consists of a 6-year primary sequence followed by a 4-year junior secondary school, and topped by a 3-4-year senior secondary cycle. The 3 year program leads to the "Baccalaureate" while the 4-year program leads to a certificate gained through a competitive exam. Secondary technical and professional education is offered in separate schools. While there is no university in the country, there are a few institutions of post secondary education including a polytechnic and the Institute of Higher Islamic Studies. Most students seeking higher education go abroad, often financed by Arab speaking nations in the Middle East.

Function

When independence came in 1960, there were few formally educated citizens in the northern area. Educational opportunity is now slowly developing in this region. As part of its Islamization program the government strongly encourages Arabic as the principal language of instruction. However, because of complaints from the minority in the south, the use of French also is permitted. The teaching of indigenous traditions has been revived through the primary school curriculum. The curriculum also includes a strong emphasis on Arabic studies. The government is endeavoring to bring formal education to the nomads through the introduction of tent schools that follow the groups.

NIGER

Overview

Geographically the country is the largest in West Africa. However, with 90% of its population engaged in nomadic livestock activities or agriculture it has been difficult for the government to deliver educational services. The problem is compounded by a serious drought condition throughout the Sahel. The government pursues a twin policy of educational expansion and equalization. Special efforts are made to provide women and the rural population with schooling. Still, by the mid-1980's the illiteracy rate among the adult population was over 85%. With the recent increase in uranium and coal production the government is now spending more on education.

Structure

The Ministry of Education is responsible for directing most formal education through the secondary and technical level. However, the Ministry of Rural Economy is responsible for agricultural education while the Ministry of Health directs the education of nurses. As is the case in most former French colonies, the system is highly centralized with the national ministry managing by means of regional and district offices. The basic structure consists of a 6-year primary cycle that is now compulsory, followed by a 4-year junior and 3-year senior secondary sequence. External examinations dictate progress up the educational ladder. Expansion of opportunity at all levels has been handicapped by the lack of qualified indigenous teachers. The University of Niamey emerged in the mid-1970's and is now an important research center in West Africa.

Function

Movement away from the French model began soon after independence and continues today. In rural areas teachers are viewed as community leaders as well as school teachers. Liberal use of radio and television is being used in efforts to bring schooling to rural citizens. Special attention is given to literacy campaigns to combat the high illiteracy rate. Recently the government expanded vocational and technical education to help prepare the youth for participation in the growing mining industry.

NIGERIA

Overview

The nation is often seen as the most dominant and complex in West Africa if not all of Africa. It is also one of the richest. With a population of over 120 million it is the largest on the continent and as an oil exporting nation in the 1980's its economic potential has been discovered.

The complexity evolves from the more then 350 language groups within its boundaries and from a federal government that shares power and money with state governments. The rivalries between federal and state government officials is matched by the rivalries between religious and ethnic groups seeking political and economic influence. The continuous quest for more schooling by its citizens often has permitted education to move beyond the divisive interests of political leaders.

Structure

The adminstration is shared between the federal and state governments. The National Council on Education and the Joint Consultative Committee on Education are the two bodies that attempt to ensure uniform practices throughout the country. Membership in the two bodies includes federal and state ministers and commissioners of education. In addition there is a federal inspectorate service that attempts to develop equal standards. The federal Ministry of Education sets national policy and coordinates the financing of the system. Each state has a ministry of education that manages its primary and secondary schools as well as its teachers' colleges. The states also formulate the curriculum and administer examinations. In some states local school committees assume some responsibility for managing their schools. Since the 1975-80 National Development Plan, federal involvement is increasing. The plan views education as an instrument that should promote national unity and reduce regional imbalances. Toward that end, "universal primary education" has been introduced and financed by the federal government. The federal government also finances the training of additional teachers needed to implement its plan.

The present system includes 6 years of compulsory primary school and a proposal for 3 years of junior and 3 years of senior secondary school. The 3-3 plan replaces a 5-year secondary school that included a 2-year "sixth form" based on the British model. The overall system is oriented toward examinations at each level that will determine who moves forward. The best known examination is that administered by the West African Examination Council. Their examination sets the standard for most of the previous British colonies in West Africa.

Vocational education is organized at the secondary level and technical education takes place in the nation's 18 polytechnics or colleges of technology that offer courses which vary from one to four years. By the mid-1980's there were 16 federal and 8 state universities all financed by the federal government and administered through the National Universities Commission. The autonomy of the universities is slowly being eroded by federal involvement which is attempting to move higher education toward programs that meet national manpower needs.

Function

The Nigerianization of the curriculum is a hall mark of the formal system. In part this is being accomplished through the National Book Development Council which produces textbooks by Nigerian authors. A 1977 White Paper on education also emphasizes the study of Nigerian culture in order to promote national unity. The language of instruction for the first 3 years is in the mother tongue. After that all instruction is in English. In some urban areas primary education begins in the English language.

In the north, where the Islamic religion is pervasive, Koranic schools exert a strong influence and receive a small state subsidy. The primary schools tend to be found in neighborhoods and teach the first 10 chapters of the Koran. At the secondary level students are taught Islamic studies.

Recently educational development throughout the nation is being slowed by the reduction in the amount of money available through oil exportation. There is some doubt whether the economy can diversify to the extent necessary to continue educational expansion.

SENEGAL

Overview

Senegal was the oldest French colony in Africa and its capital, Dakar, served as the administrative center for all ten of France's colonies. As a consequence the city was viewed as a showpiece of colonialism and the starting point for educational development. Prior to independence Senegal had Francophone's only university. It also contained the principal higher educational institutions in the form of technical, vocational and teacher training institutions as well as the only two "lycees" in the French colonies. One result of this was a core of well educated citizens at the time of independence. Another result was the rejection of things "French" when the new government took over. For several years the nation led the way in introducing the concept of "Negritude" into its schools and championed African literature, the arts and music.

Structure

The lack of finances has caused the government to shorten primary education from 6 to 5 years and move slowly on the implementation of its universal primary education law. Recently primary schools introduced two daily shifts in an attempt to cut costs and to provide more places for students. Entrance into secondary schools is through a highly competitive exam. The first tier of secondary education lasts 4 years and is available to approximately 10-15 % of the eligible youth. Another competitive examination determines the direction of further education after the first 4 years. The academically talented proceed to 3 additional years of an academic curriculum that leads to high education. Others go to teacher training, technical or vocational schools where the majority of students still in school terminate their formal education.

The system is administered by the Ministry of Education which has complete control over primary, secondary and higher education. The Ministry of Technical and Vocational Training is responsible in these areas while the Ministry of Popular Education, Youth, and Sports supervises practical and adult education. All of the ministries work through the country's eight regions and 27 departments and utilize a series of school inspectors. In a nation that is approximately 85% Muslim there is a parallel system of Koranic schools. Recently these schools have become more popular because of a growing criticism that traditional values are disappearing.

Function

There are three major issues that affect the way schools function. First is the criticism of the high drop out rate at the primary level. There are several reasons for this wastage, but the two most often noted are the difficulty children have with the French language and the high standards of the schools. It is estimated that only 15% of the overall population can read and write in French. A second issue surrounds the dual demand to Africanize the schools while simultaneously teaching an academic curriculum that leads to a competitive exam. The balance of these two demands has created an on-going problem. The third issue deals with higher education, the students selected and the curriculum they prefer. Higher education can lead to a diploma, a license, or a degree. Added pressure for more higher education led to the opening of a second university in 1979. However, in spite of government attempts to direct students into career paths in areas needed for national development, there is now a growing problem of unemployed graduates of higher educational institutions who have specialized in the liberal arts.

SIERRA LEONE

Overview

The uniqueness of the country lies in its historical background. This former British colony was populated by freed slaves from England, Canada, and the Caribbean who set up their own city state around the harbor called Freetown. One consequence was a British colony with one set of laws for the many ethnic groups in the hinterland and another set of laws for the people around Freetown who spoke their own language, Creole, and had their own economy based on trade. With independence the educational challenge was to introduce Western education into the rural, agricultural based interior. For the most part the challenge still remains. The illiteracy rate is estimated to be around 75% of the adult population.

Structure

In principle the control of formal education resides in the Ministry of Education, but in reality there is a partnership between the church related voluntary bodies and the government. The voluntary bodies liaise with the Ministry through their educational secretaries for both primary and secondary education. One consequence is three categories of schools: (1) government schools administered by the government; (2) government assisted schools that have their own board of governors and were developed by Christian missionaries; and (3) private institutions often administered by the church. All schools must follow a government curriculum and adhere to the same educational ladder. Primary education is 6 years in duration although some communities provide an additional year to prepare students for the entrance examination into secondary school. Yearly examinations at the primary level lead to a large drop-out problem. The secondary schools are patterned after the British model with the most prestigious operated by Christian missionary groups. Five years of secondary school lead to the West African Examination Council's ordinary level examination and an additional Form 6 leads to the advanced level examination and entrance into the university. There are four trade and technical institutes and several teacher training colleges, but the prestige resides in the University of Sierra Leone with its two colleges. One of the colleges, Fourah Bay, dates back to 1823 when it was the center of higher education for British colonial West Africa. Many of the civil servants and business people throughout the area were educated there. The second college, Njala University College, was developed along the lines of an American land-grant college.

Function

The Ministry supplies primary schools with a syllabus. In spite of several attempts to make the curriculum more practical in its orientation, formal subjects still dominate. The failure is placed on poorly trained teachers and missionary dominated schools. The secondary level also is dominated by academic subjects and as a consequence the students around Freetown do especially well. Often rural families do not see the benefits of an English language education. Recently attempts are being made to introduce more practical sciences and agriculture into both the primary and secondary schools. A UNESCO supported "Bunumbu Project" in the 1970's and 80's gained an international reputation for developing indigenous teaching and learning programs for rural schools. The curriculum was developed by rural educators and, in part, was developed to produce teachers for rural schools. Unfortunately, once trained many of the teachers left the rural areas.

TOGO

Overview

Since independence from France the Republic has made steady educational progress in spite of being one of the poorest nations in the world based on its gross national product. Its educational development has been aided by a small elite group of bilingual citizens and an indigenous teaching staff. The bilingualism in English and French is due to its proximity to Ghana. During the 60's and 70's Togolese crossed the border in relatively large numbers where entrance to secondary and higher education was much easier to obtain. The bilingualism in German and French is due to the large number of scholarships offered to the Togolese by the German government. Until the end of World War I Togo was a German colony and ties remain, primarily in the form of financial aid.

Structure

The system remains patterned after the French. It is an examination oriented, centrally administered system that is producing a small group of elite Togolese. The Ministry of National Education functions through four directorates that are responsibile for all phases of the educational ladder. They are assisted by a series of inspectors who travel to the five regions and make periodic reports. The educational ladder consists of a 6-year primary level followed by a 4-year academic junior school or a 3-4-year vocational-technical preparation program. Ninety percent of the students are in the academic track. Senior secondary schools are 3 years in duration and prepare students for the "Baccalaureate" and entrance to higher education. In 1970 the government opened the University of Benin, but quite a few students receive their higher education outside the country.

The government is faced with a high illiteracy rate and the difficulty of bringing education to rural areas. As a consequence it has introduced a series of functional literacy campaigns closely allied to skill development and consciousness raising.

Function

The large increase in primary school enrollment coincides with the government's campaign in "authenticity" which promotes indigenous values and languages. Still, French remains the basic language of instruction at all levels and is one cause of the large drop-out rate. Another is the cost of school fees and the purchase price of imported textbooks. The secondary school curriculum does pay some attention to African literature. The technical and vocational schools offer theoretical and practical preparation with successful students receiving a state diploma in their field of study.

Recent developments include an emphasis on the teaching of science by means of better prepared teachers and the development of laboratories. More attention also is being paid to the improvement of technical education through the establishment of training centers linked to various corporations.

BIBLIOGRAPHY

Adesina, Segun and Segun Ogunsaju, eds. *Secondary Education in Nigeria*. Ile-Ife: University of Ife Press Ltd., 1984.

Bray, Mark, Peter B. Clarke and David Stephens. *Education and Society in Africa*. London: Edward Arnold (Publishers) Ltd., 1986.

Cameron, John, ed. *International Handbook of Educational Systems*, Volume II. Chichester: John Wiley and Sons, 1983.

deLusignan, Guy. *French Speaking Africa Since Independence*. New York: Frederick A. Praeger, 1969.

Fafunwa, A. Babs and J.U. Aisiku, eds. *Education in Africa: A Comparative Survey*. London: George Allen and Unwin, 1982.

Farja, Abdulatif Hussein. *International Yearbook of Education*, Volume XL-1988. Paris: UNESCO, 1988.

Hawes, Hugh. *Curriculum and Reality in African Primary Schools*. Burnt Mill: Longman Group Ltd., 1979.

Husen, Torsten and T. Neville Postlethwaite, eds. *The International Encyclopedia of Education*. Oxford: Pergamon Press Ltd., 1985.

Kurian, George T., ed. *World Education Encyclopedia*. New York: Facts on File Publications, 1988.

UNESCO. *The Educational Process and Historiography in Africa*. Paris: UNESCO, 1985.

World Bank. *Education in Sub-Saharan Africa*. Washington, D.C.: The World Bank, 1988.

ANNOTATED BIBLIOGRAPHY

History and Philosophy

Books

78.   Adaralegbe, Adeniji, ed. *A Philosophy for Nigerian Education*.
       Ibadan: Heinemann Educational Books (Nigeria) Ltd., 1972.

Contains the proceedings of the Nigerian National Curriculum
Conference held in 1969 and sponsored by the National Educational
Research Council. Nigerian authors discuss the purpose of education
at the primary, secondary, college and university levels. Attention
also is given to the education of women and the role of scientific and
technological education. A summary of recommendations from the
conference is included as well as a collection of detailed memoranda
submitted to the conference delegates by leading educators.

79.   Agbodeka, Francis. *Achimota in the National Setting*. Accra:
       AFRAM Publications Ltd., 1977.

The book was published as part of the institution's celebration of its
first fifty years.   The activities, anecdotes, internal politics and
educational accomplishments are discussed from an insider's
perspective. The author interviewed quite a few graduates which
added a great deal to the study.

80.   Enobakhare, G.N.I.   *How Shall We Educate?*   Lagos:
       Macmillan and Co. Ltd., 1971.

The author's thoughts and opinions on the goals and objectives of
education in Nigeria. One major question addressed in "how can
education help the individual Nigerian to rediscover his personality
and to contribute to the human resources of the whole country?"
Formal education at all levels is briefly discussed.

81.   Fafunwa, A. Babs. *History of Education in Nigeria*. London:
       George Allen and Unwin Ltd., 1974.

Traces the overall evolution of education through specific historical
periods. Special emphasis is given to traditional education in the past
and present, and the administration and structure of education since
independence. Chapters also are devoted to Muslim and Christian
education as well as education during the colonial era. A highly
respected author who shows special insight.

82.   Graham, C.K. *The History of Education in Ghana*. London:

82. Graham, C.K. *The History of Education in Ghana.* London: Frank Cass and Company Ltd., 1971.

Highlights the growth and development of European-styled education in the Gold Coast from the beginning of Western contact to Ghanian independence in 1957. Chapters are devoted to agricultural and vocational training, girls' education and teacher training. Some comparisons are made with the content and organization of education in England.

83. Kelly, Gail P. *"When I Become a Fonctionnaire:" School Knowledge in French West Africa, 1918-1938.* Buffalo: Comparative Education Center, State University of New York at Buffalo, 1984.

One of a series of "Occasional" papers produced by the Comparative Education Center. The paper presents a set of original text and student materials which helps to reveal the reality of the curriculum and of student life in French Colonial Africa. The introductory essay provides statistics and information on the structure of formal education. An excellent example of material which helps to explain classroom teaching and activities during the colonial period.

84. McWilliam, H. O. A. and M. A. Kwamena-Poh. *The Development of Education in Ghana.* London: Longman Group Ltd., 1975.

A brief history of the nation's educational system primarily for use by teachers in training. The book is an update of an earlier version and contains reference to educational development after independence as well as an opening chapter on education in traditional society. It is quite detailed with special reference to government reports.

85. Mumford, W. Bryant. *Africans Learn to be French.* New York: Negro University's Press, 1970.

Reviews educational activities in the former seven colonies of French West Africa based upon a tour of the area in 1935. The book was reprinted in 1970. It contains some interesting observations by the author as well as some predictions that failed to materialize.

86. Nnolim, Charles, ed. *The Role of Education in Contemporary Africa.* New York: Professors World Peace Academy, 1988.

Chronicles the proceedings of the Professors World Peace Academy conferences held in Nigeria in October, 1983 and June, 1984.

87.   Ocho, Lawrence. *Education in Northern Nigeria.* London: George Allen and Unwin Ltd., 1981.

88.   Ozigi, Albert and Lawrence Ocho. *Education in Northern Nigeria.* London: George Allen and Unwin Ltd., 1981.

Traces the historical development of education beginning with the influence of Islamic and Christian educators, through the colonial period, and into developments after independence. Attention is given to the administration and structure of the schools as well as the changing goals during different historical periods. Some thought is given to the problems which evolved after independence.

Articles

89.   Adams, Milton and Medjoma, Coulibaly. "African Traditional Pedagogy in a Modern Perspective." *Prospects* 15, No. 2 (1985): 275-80.

Identified pedagogical principles of African traditional education and tests their use in schools located in rural villages of the Ivory Coast. Finds ten major principles being used in the schools today.

90.   Obidi, S.S. "Indigenous Moral Education in Nigeria." *Journal of Moral Education* 13, No. 1 (1984): 56-60.

Discusses how Nigerian children experience moral education from the family and the community through direct instruction and observation. They learn that gods and ancestors are a source of human morality.

91.   Omatseye, J. Nesin. "The Essence of a Liberal Education in Nigeria." *Journal of General Education* 33, No. 4 (1982): 263-72.

Answers critics of the liberal arts legacy from the colonial period by relating it to the contributions of traditional education. Advocates an educational system with a balance between liberal arts, science and technical education.

Education and Development

Books

92.   Adesina, Segun and Tinuke L. Johnson. *Cost-Benefit Analysis of Education in Nigeria.* Lagos: Lagos University Press, 1981.

93. Adesina, Segun. *The Development of Modern Education in Nigeria*. Ibadan: Heinemann Educational Books Ltd., 1988.

A comprehensive and far ranging account of the development of education until 1983. The author builds his chapters around four important features: (1) the rapidity of the educational systems growth; (2) the overwhelming influence of politics; (3) the apparent failure of the educational system to respond positively to the social and economic demands of the nation; and (4) the inability over the years to determine who should pay for education. A very detailed book which is well documented. Good use of statistics.

94. Adeyanju, Thomas K. *Educational Research in the Northern Nigeria States: An Annotated Bibliography of Students' Theses and Projects*. Zaria, Nigeria: S.N., 1980.

95. Anyanwu, C. Nnorom. *Community Education and Development: The Experience in West Africa*. Ibadan: Abiprint Publishing Co. Ltd., 1982.

Focuses on Anglophone West Africa with chapters devoted to specific roles community education has undertaken. Examples include Ghana, where it was used to satisfy a growing demand for formal education, Nigeria, where it ushered in a mass literacy campaign, and the Gambia, where it helped in the search for self-reliance. Chapters also discuss the scope of community education and link it to the adult and nonformal education movements in West Africa.

96. Boblibaugh, Jerry B. *Educational Development in Guinea, Mali, Senegal, and Ivory Coast*. Washington, D.C.: U.S. Government Printing Office, 1972.

Describes the educational system and discusses major trends and problems since independence in four Francophone West African countries. A brief sketch is offered of the different levels of formal education. A concluding chapter offers some comparisons among the four countries.

97. Carr-Hill, R. and G. Rosengart. *Education in Guinea-Bissau, 1978-1981*. Stockholm: Swedish International Development Authority, 1982.

One of a series of documents produced by the Education Division which highlights education programs sponsored by the Swedish government.

98.   Edem, D.A. *Introduction to Educational Administration in Nigeria.* Ibadan: Spectrum Books, 1982.

99.   Eitm, James and Onwokwe Alaezi, eds. *Relevance in Nigerian Education: Patterns, Approaches and Strategies.* Ibadan: University Press Ltd., 1988.

A series of articles which emanated from a 1986 National Workshop on Relevance in Nigerian Education organized by the University of Jos Faculty of Education. The articles highlighted need-based teaching and learning strategies, a better and redefined relationship between the dominant academic curriculum and practical skills and the "needed" implementation strategies. The chapters are written by Nigerians who spent some time attempting to interpret the definition of relevance.

100.   Etuk, J.D. *Government and Education: Study of the Role of Government in the Educational Policies, Administration, and Problems in Nigeria.* Calabar: Paico Press and Books, 1984.

101.   Johnson, P. and Others. *Ghanian Education, 1957-1972: An Annotated Bibliography.* London: Institute of Education, University of London, 1974.

Articles

102.   Enaohwo, J. Okpako. "An Ideology of Educational Planning in Nigeria." *Journal of Educational Thought* 18, No. 3 (1984): 162-67.

Advocates the process of systematic forward planning guided by an ideology. The author finds the Nigerian National Policy on Education too abstract and unattainable and cites reasons why.

103.   Enaohwo, J. Okpako. "Education and the National Economy of Nigeria." *International Social Science Journal* 37, No. 2 (1985):   237-46.

Discusses the important role education has played in the economic development of the country; sees a strong relationship between the two.

104.   Harber, C.R. "Development and Political Attitudes: The Role of Schooling in Northern Nigeria." *Comparative Education* 20, Vol. 3 (1984):   387-403.

Discusses factors which influence the development of political attitudes of Hausa primary and secondary students in Kano State. Describes influences in terms of attitudes toward citizenship, authority and political participation.

105. Kone, Zobila. "The Ways in Which Technology is Imported and Their Effects on Employment and Training: The Case of the Ivory Coast." *Prospects* 14, No. 4 (1984): 509-21.

Argues that an educational policy is needed to improve the nation's ability to assimilate and adapt imported technology and produce local technology.

106. Oni, Bankole. "Education and Alternative Avenues of Mobility: A Nigerian Study." *Comparative Education Review* 32, No. 1 (1988): 87-99.

Attempts to show how the apprenticeship system functions as competition to formal education. Ten villages were studied to determine alternative economic opportunities in relation to the level of modernization in each village. The study concludes that the value of formal education relates to the lack of alternative opportunities within the village economy.

107. Oyeneye, O.Y. "Educational Planning and Self-Allocation: An Example from Nigeria." *Comparative Education* 16, No. 2 (1980): 129-37.

Surveys primary school leavers' aspirations to examine the self-allocation potential of Nigeria's attempt to vocationalize its lower educational system. Relates educational planning to self-allocation and the ability of new institutions to attract students to meet their educational and occupational goals.

108. McDowell, David W. "The Impact of the National Policy of Education on Indigenous Education in Nigeria." *International Review of Education* 28, No. 1 (1980): 49-64.

Suggests that the quick implementation of the national policy would regulate indigenous private education and craft apprenticeships and as a consequence aggravate the employment situation.

Primary Education

Books

109.   Boakye, J. Kwasi Ayim and John Oxenham. *Qualifications and Quality of Education in Ghanian Rural Middle Schools*. Brighton: Institute of Development Studies, University of Sussex, 1982.

The report is one of a group which flows from a collective research project entitled, "Qualifications and Selection in Educational Systems." The study was done in collaboration with the University of Cape Coast Department of Sociology. Six rural middle schools formed the sample for the study. The purpose was to assess whether the desire for qualifications for jobs in the modern, salaried sector of the economy undermined the achievement of good education as defined by the Ministry of Education and the Ghana Education Service.

110.   Bray, Mark. *Universal Primary Education in Nigeria: A Study of Kano State*. London: Routledge and Kegan Paul, 1981.

Describes the build-up to the campaign of universal primary education in this northern state as well as the first four years of its operation. A national perspective is added to the movement as well as a detailed account of its relationship to the formal system in Kano State. Attention also is paid to the movment's social and economic impact. The author taught in Kano during the inception of the campaign and was able to come in contact with many of the educators responsible for its implementation.

111.   Oyedeji, Lekan. *Universal Primary Education in Nigeria: Its Implications for National Development*. Lagos: Lagos University Press, 1983.

Articles

112.   Obidi, S.S. "Northern Nigeria and the Issue of Free Universal Primary Education." *Journal of Negro Education* 57, No. 1 (1988):   94-105.

113.   Ogundare, Samuel F.   "Curriculum Development: A Description of the Development of the National Curriculum for Primary School Studies in Nigeria." *Educational Studies* 14, No. 1 (1988):   43-50.

Secondary Education

Books

114.	Adesina, Segun and Segun Ogunsaju, eds. *Secondary Education in Nigeria*. Ile-Ife: University of Ife Press, 1984.

Describes the existing and anticipated problems brought about by the rapid increase in the number of secondary schools. Topics include sociological, and psychological issues as well as concerns related to finances and management. Chapters are written by Nigerians involved with secondary and higher education.

115.	Institute of Education. *Introducing Curriculum Revision in English in Sierra Leone*. Freetown: University of Sierra Leone, 1973.

Report of 1973 conference which brought together the educational leaders and policy makers to meet with the secondary school teachers of English. The objective was to introduce new revisions to the teachers who would have to implement them. The report contained a preliminary working paper, the conference papers, which introduced approaches to the new curriculum, reports from conference working parties and conference resolutions.

Articles

116.	Bolarini, T.A. "National Policy on Education: Implication on the Junior Secondary School for Rural Development in Nigeria." *Kenya Journal of Education* 3, No. 1 (1986) 85-111.

Describes the new national policy which divides the secondary school into two phases each lasting three years. The junior secondary school is composed of prevocational and academic courses while the senior secondary is comprehensive in its curriculum.

117.	Idowu, Adeyemi and Abimbade Dere. "Socioeconomic Status and Occupational Aspirations of High School Seniors in Nigeria." *Journal of Employment Counseling* 20, No. 4 (1983): 186-92.

Results of a study shows that students with a higher socioeconomic status had a higher occupational aspiration level. Suggests that career guidance be used to help other students.

118.	Okoye, Mary. "Community Secondary Schools: A Case Study of Nigerian Innovation in Self-Help." *International Journal of Educational Development* 6, No. 4 (1986): 263-74.

Tertiary and Higher Education

Books

119.   Aminu, Jibril M.   *Quality and Stress in Nigerian Education.*
Maiduguri and Zaria: University of Maiduguri and Northern
Nigerian Publishing Co., 1986.

The author is a distinguished Nigerian educator who has been Vice
Chancellor of the University of Maidugori and Federal Minister of
Education. The book is a collection of his selected addresses and
papers. The focus is on University development with sections devoted
to management, funding, technological education and international
cooperation.

120.   Ayandele, E.A.   *The Educated Elite in the Nigerian Society.*
Ibadan: University Press, 1974.

Series of university lectures delivered by the author previous to the
25th Anniversary Celebration of the founding of the University of
Ibadan. The lectures record the shortcomings of some of Nigeria's
past leaders.   The author defines the educated elite as the
Western-style literate groups. He looks at them, with irreverence,
during the four periods of modern Nigerian history.

121.   Barkan, Joel D.   *An African Dilemma: University Students,
Development and Politics in Ghana, Tanzania and Uganda.*
Nairobi: Oxford University Press, 1975.

Attempts to present a broad overview of the different roles students
are expected to play in three different countries. The author surveyed
1900 students and analyzed their perceptions on such topics as
national integration, economic development and the political
dimensions of students' expected roles as part of a new elite.

122.   Chizea, Chinelo Amaka, ed.   *Twenty Years of University
Education in Nigeria.* Washington,D.C.: Nigerian Universities
Commission, 1983.

123.   Fafunwa, A. Babs.   *A History of Nigerian Higher Education.*
Lagos: Macmillan and Co. Ltd., 1971.

Offers a perspective on higher education within the context of
national development. Government and nongovernment reports are
used as vantage points to analyze and evaluate higher education.
Chapters also are devoted to the administration and financing of

higher education as well as its students, staff and curriculum. The author's first introduction to the topic was through his Ph.D. thesis at New York University.

124. Okafor, Nduka. *The Development of Universities in Nigeria.* London: Camelot Press Ltd., 1971.

Chronicles the development of specific universities during the period 1868-1967. Special emphasis is placed on the role of political influence. References include government reports, legislative council debates, newspaper accounts and recognized books in the field. At times, quite detailed.

125. Osuntokun, Akinjide. *Expansion of University Education in Nigeria.* Washington, D.C.: Nigerian Universities Commission, 1982.

Articles

126. Arubayi, Eric. "A Comparative Study of Academic Performance in Teacher Education Curricula in Nigeria." *Journal of General Education* 38, No. 3 (1986): 211-20.

Compares and evaluates two tracks for teacher training. Reviews the performance of students in a science education curricula who complete a program leading to the Nigerian Certificate of Education in contrast to the performance of students in a noncertificate program.

127. Banya, Kingsley. "The Role of International Organizations in Aid: A Case Study of a Teacher Education Programme in Sierra Leone." *International Review of Education* 34, No. 3 (1988): 477-94.

128. Bloom, Leonard and Howard Woodhouse. "Nigerian Higher Education: Policy and Practice." *Canadian and International Education* 17, No. 2 (1988): 5-21.

129. Enahwo, J.O. "Financing in Nigeria and Implications for Higher Education." *Journal of Educational Administration and History* 12, No. 1 (1980): 46-53.

Examines the role of the government in financing universities and the effect it has on the development, governance and control of the universities.

130.   Hatt, D.G. "Response to 'Nigerian Higher Education' -- A Critique of the Liberal Position." *Canadian and International Education* 17, No. 2 (1988): 22-27.

131.   McCain, James A. "Educational Development and Higher Education in Ghana." *Journal of Negro Education* 49, No. 1 (1980): 91-96.

Discusses ways in which higher education can contribute to national development and suggests ways in which development may be helped by university resources.

132.   Obah, Thelma. "Readings in Higher Education in Nigeria: Problems and Progress." *Journal of Reading* 25, No. 4 (1982): 315-21.

Describes the problems facing developmental reading instruction, their causes and possible solutions.

133.   Obasi, Emma. "The Social Origins of Student Teachers in Nigeria." *Journal of Education for Teaching* 13, No. 2 (1987): 177-81.

A survey of 578 bachelor of education students randomly chosen from three universities to determine their social origins.

134.   Olaitan, S.O. "The Status of Teacher Education in Nigeria: A Challenge for Improvement." *Improving College and University Teaching* 31, No. 4 (1983): 176-82.

Proposes a plan to improve the curriculum of teacher education. Focuses on instructional quality and the relationship of the curriculum to student achievement.

135.   Olukoya, A. "Teaching Medical Teachers How to Teach in Lagos, Nigeria." *Medical Teacher* 8, No. 2 (1986): 145-48.

Discusses a program designed to improve the teaching skills of medical school teachers. Describes a workshop designed to provide skills in curriculum design, audio-visual aids, knowledge assessment, simulations and the writing of objectives.

136.   Osunde, Egerton. "American Influences in Curriculum Reforms in African Universities: An Analysis of Innovations in Nigerian Universities." *Journal of Abstracts in International Education* 15, No. 1 (1986): 25-35.

137.   Osunde,Egerton and David P. Ellis.   "Teacher Education in Nigeria: An Evolving Academic System."   *International Education* 15, No. 2 (1986):   63-68.

138.   Woodhouse, Howard R.   "Power and the University in a Developing Country: Nigeria and Cultural Dependency." *Compare* 17, No. 2 (1987):   119-36.

Examines cultural dependence and the way in which university education enhances such dependency by promoting the process of elite formation. Suggests an alternative model.

Specialized Education (Adult, Community, Nonformal, Technical, Vocational)

Books

139.   Anyanwu, C. Nnorum.   *Community Education and Development: The Experience in West Africa*. Ibadan: Abiprint Publishing Co., 1982.

140.   Brown, Lalage and S.H. Olutomori, eds. *A Handbook of Adult Education for West Africa*.   London: Hutchinson and Co. (Publishers) Ltd., 1979.

Designed to be a practical handbook for those engaged in adult education. Chapters are devoted to the planning, implementation and evaluation of adult education as well as methods and materials which can be used. Special attention is given to education in rural areas. The 1976 UNESCO recommendations on the development of adult education are appended.

141.   Dankwah, James.   *Vocational Training in Ghana: Towards a Modality of its Development*. Aachen: Rader Verlag, 1987.

142.   Ezeomah, Chimah.   *Nomadic Education in Nigeria: The Fulani*. Driffield, England: Nafferton Books Ltd., 1983.

Presents a detailed view of the migrant Fulani and their way of life. Attempts to develop a strategy for integrating education into their way of life without abandoning Fulani culture. The author shows good insight into the culture.

143.   Greenstreet, Miranda.   *Females in the Agricultural Labour Force and Nonformal Education for Rural Development in Ghana*. The Hague: Institute of Social Studies, 1981.

144.   Okedara, J.T.   *A Comparative Study of Formal and Non-Formal Educational Wastages in Ibadan, Nigeria.* Ibadan: Institute of Education, University of Ibadan, 1981.

145.   Okeem, E.O.   *Adult Education in Ghana and Tanzania, 1945-1975.* Nsukka: University of Nigeria Press, 1982.

Discusses the socio-cultural determinants of literacy education and extramural studies.

146.   Omolewa, Michael.   *Adult Education Practice in Nigeria.* Ibadan: Evans Brothers Press, 1981.

Articles

147.   Anyanwu, Clement N.   "The Agricultural Radio Clubs in the Republic of Benin: A Case Study of Agricultural Diffusion in West Africa."   *Journal of International and Comparative Education* 1, No. 3 (1986): 751-75.

148.   Fiah, Solomon.   "Education, Rural Small Scale Industries and Employment in Ghana."   *Compare* 18, No. 2 (1988): 139-52.

149.   Fieldhouse, Roger.   "Cold War and Colonial Conflicts in British West African Adult Education, 1947-1953."   *History of Education Quarterly* 24, No. 3 (1984): 359-71.

Traces the introduction of adult education in British colonies by educators.   Examines the position that the programs offered more support to the progressive views of the African independence movements than to the colonialists' conservative policies.

150.   Fofana, Amara.   "Education and Productive Work in Guinea."   *Prospects* 12, No. 4 (1982): 477-83.

Discusses the education centers in Guinea which provided education and work experience for students from primary through post-secondary education.   The structure, educational resources and social impact of the centers are described.   They are designed to teach scientific and technical knowledge and to serve as production units.

151.   Hamilton, Edwin.   "Adult Education and Community Development in Nigeria."   *Graduate Studies Journal* 2 (1984): 63-75.

152. Kogoe, Akrima. "Trends and Issues in Vocational Technical Education in Francophone West Africa." *Journal of Studies in Technical Careers* 7, No. 2 (1985): 81-90.

Emphasizes the need for a strong commitment to vocational technical education as a means and goal of development. Suggests that the public policies on education must shift to meet the demands of modern technology.

153. Malamah-Thomas, David H. "Community Theatre With and By the People: The Sierra Leone Experience." *Convergence* 20, No. 1 (1987): 59-68.

Focuses on the Theatre for Development Program designed to use community theatre to teach about health and community development activities.

154. Okeem, E. Odinakaschuku. "An Assessment by Adult Education Personnel of the Problems of Adult Education Programmes in Selected States of Nigeria, 1976-1982." *International Journal of Lifelong Education* 4, No. 3 (1985): 239-57.

Advocates adult education as a necessary supplement to formal education. Identifies the major obstacles to adult education programs found throughout the selected States.

155. Omolewa, Michael. "Mass Literacy Campaigns in Nigeria: 1940-1960." *Indian Journal of Adult Education* 41, No. 9 (1980): 15-23.

Chronicles the history of several literacy campaigns. Emphasizes the importance of education outside the school in order to bring about social, political and economic change.

156. Osuji, E. "The University and Community Service in Nigeria." *Adult Education* (London) 57, No. 3 (1984): 244-51.

Describes the extent of extension activities undertaken by the Department of Adult Education at the University of Ibadan. Examines specific community development activities and the organization of community services.

157. Ouane, Adama. "The Experience of Mali in Training Literacy Workers." *Convergence* 19, No. 1 (1986): 13-14.

158.   Oyeneye, O.Y.   "The Problem of Self-Allocation in the Planning of Vocational Education in Nigeria." *Vocational Aspect of Education* 32, No. 82 (1980): 39-43.

Discusses how the self-allocation process of students can undermine the planning of vocational education.   Describes the research conducted on students' attitudes toward skilled jobs and craft-based education.

159.   Peretomode, Victor and Ayuba A. Maigari.   "Vo-Tech in Northern Nigeria." *Canadian Vocational Journal* 2, No. 3 (1985): 15-19.

Examines the qualifications, teaching experience and industrial training of the teachers in vocational schools.   Raises such questions as, what is the nature of the curriculum, what kind of equipment is available and what are the class sizes attending lectures?

160.   Robertston, Claire C.   "Formal or Nonformal Education? Entrepreneurial Women in Ghana." *Comparative Education Review* 28, No. 4 (1984): 639-58.

Surveys 42 Central Accra schoolgirls, and 42 women engaged in selling, to determine the relationship between formal education and marketing skills.   Formal education proved neither to be helpful in promoting trading knowledge nor in providing the skills necessary to get a job.

161.   Turrittin, Jane.   "Integrated Literacy in Mali." *Comparative Education Review* 33, No. 1 (1989): 59-76.

Focuses on the promotion of literacy in conjunction with work-related activities.   Literacy practices in the classroom and outside the formal structure are explored as is the use of the teacher as a literacy leader. Provides a detailed illustration of an ethnographic study which examines the promotion of integrated literacy in rural Mali.

162.   Urch, George E.   "Nonformal Education and Rural Development in Ghana." *International Journal of Educational Development* 4, No. 4 (1984): 305-314.

Describes and evaluates a nonformal education project that evolved through a collaborative arrangement between a private voluntary organization in Ghana and a North American University.   Specific kinds of facilitator training are identified in order to determine those which increase rural villagers' ability to implement development activities. Analyzes what appears to work and problems in implementation.

Curriculum and Methods

Books

163. Bamgbose, Ayo, ed. *Mother Tongue Education: The West African Experience*. Paris: UNESCO Press, 1976.

Commissioned under UNESCO's Anthropology and Language Science in Educational Development Program, the book was designed to give educators and policy makers a narrative account of developments in selected West African countries. Three broad areas are covered: (1) situations where preparations are being made to introduce the mother tongue into the formal school systems; (2) the state of affairs where there has been a long tradition of mother tongue education; and (3) special projects and experimentation.

164. Mgbodile, T.O., ed. *Issues in Teacher Education and Science Curriculum in Nigeria*. Nigeria: The Organization, 1986.

Articles

165. Ale, Sam O. "Difficulties Facing Mathematics Teachers in Developing Countries -- A Case Study of Nigeria." *Educational Studies in Mathematics* 12, No. 4 (1981): 479-89.

Examines the current problems of school and university mathematics as they relate to teachers. A large expansion in mathematics teachers' education programs is viewed as a necessity.

166. Awoniyi, Adedeji and Florence Ala. "Effects of Alternative Language Media on Learning in Nigeria." *Journal of Negro Education* 54, No. 2 (1985): 225-31.

A study of Nigerian bilingual students (Yoruba and English) supports other research which indicates that primary education is more effective in the student's mother tongue. An experimental group taught and tested in a structured bilingual medium performed significantly better than one taught and tested in English.

167. Bamgbose, Ayo. "Education in Indigenous Languages: The West African Model of Language Education." *Journal of Negro Education* 52, No. 1 (1983): 57-64.

Contends that the West African experience supports a policy of using the mother tongue, rather than a foreign language, as the medium of instruction in schools at all levels.

168. Bamgbose, Ayo. "Mother-Tongue Medium and Scholastic Attainment in Nigeria." *Prospects* 14, No. 1 (1984): 87-93.

Evaluation of a Six Year Primary Project which shows that Nigerian students who were taught in their mother tongue (Yoruba) for the first six years of primary education scored higher academically than students who were taught in their mother tongue for the first three years and then were switched to English.

169. Danquah, Samuel A. "School Psychology in Ghana." *Journal of School Psychology* 25, No. 3 (1987): 247-53.

Describes school psychology programs beginning with the historical development of practices. Presents a comparative analysis of past and present practices. Examines the system of school administration and the professional education of teachers and psychologists.

170. d'Almeida, Irene Assiba. "The Meaning and Status of International Studies in West African Schools." *Theory and Practice* 21, No. 3 (1982): 193-99.

Emphasizes the overstressing of international studies under colonialism while indigenous traditions and languages were neglected. Suggests that educational reforms are underway to remedy the situation.

171. Egbon, Mike. "Development and Unity in Nigeria." *Media in Education and Development* 15, No. 2 (1982): 81-85.

Discusses the problems which emerged in the efforts of the government to develop a federal television system. The intentions are examined along with possible abuses.

172. Iheoma, E.O. "Moral Education in Nigeria: Problems and Prospects." *Journal of Moral Education* 14, No. 3 (1985): 183-93.

Suggests that the current approaches to moral education in the schools is inadequate to cope with the moral crisis. Recommends an integrated approach.

173. Obebe, Bolarinde. "Social Studies in the Secondary School

Curriculum in Nigeria." *Indian Social Studies Quarterly* 36, No. 2 (1983): 26-32.

Emphasizes the need to develop a social studies curriculum which will unite rather than divide the country. The difficulties in achieving this goal are examined.

174. Ojerinde, Adedibu. "Testing for the Effects of Language on Science Achievement of Primary Four Pupils in Nigeria." *Adolescence* 17, No. 66 (1982): 335-45.

Examines the effect of the medium of instruction and medium of examination on the achievement of primary school students. Students were using either Yoruba or English. Results showed that groups instructed in their mother tongue performed better.

175. Olorukooba, B.K. "An Analysis of the Function of the Arts in Primary Schools in Nigeria." *Arts Education* 38, No. 4 (1985): 13-16.

Describe how an effective arts program could assist children in understanding their culture, past and present; and in understanding people's dependence-independence balance in relation to their environment.

176. Olorundare, Solomon A. "Scientific Literacy in Nigeria: The Role of Science Education Programmes." *International Journal of Science Education* 10, No. 2 (1988): 151-58.

177. Opeola, S.M. "The Language Issue and the Use of Programed Instruction in Science Education in Nigeria." *Journal of Negro Education* 54, No. 2 (1985): 232-39.

Examines the type of programed instruction that can be used most effectively by secondary school students. Explores the relationship between English language ability and the use of programed instruction.

178. Osunde, Egerton. "Diversifying the Secondary School Curriculum in Nigeria: Problems and Policy Options." *Canadian and International Education* 17, No. 1 (1988): 36-44.

179. Owuamanam, Donatus O. "Introducing Sex Education in the Formal Education System in Nigeria." *Journal of Moral Education* 15, No. 1 (1987): 54-59.

Presents nine goals of sex education instruction and identifies problems in implementing sex education in the schools.

180.   Sawyerr, Ebun S. "The Science Curriculum and the Secondary Student in Sierra Leone." *Science Education* 69, No. 2 (1985): 147-53.

Reviews the new primary and secondary science curriculum as well as new teacher roles and instructional approaches. Results are given of the 1972-80 secondary level biology, chemistry and physics external examinations.

181.   Unolt, Solomon. "Bilingual Education in a Multilingual School System-Nigeria." *Journal of Reading* 29, No. 2 (1985): 124-30.

Empahsizes the place of language arts in a bilingual education system where English is combined with over 300 indigenous languages.

182.   Urevbu, Andrew O. "Integrating Science and Technology into a Policy of Lifelong Education in Nigeria." *International Journal of Lifelong Education* 4, No. 4 (1985): 319-25.

Discusses Nigeria's National Policy on Education in relation to science and technical education. Examines the development of vocational and technical schools, the transfer of technology and the role of research institutes. Recommendations are made.

183.   Valerien, Jean. "Education by Television in the Ivory Coast." *Educational Media International* No. 3 (1981): 11-15.

Describes the management, administration, production and broadcasting of educational television. Evaluates its use in elementary education, the training of teachers and out-of-school education during the 1970's.

Teachers

Books

184.   Marshall, Sylvia Temple. *Educational Psychology for the Teacher in Africa*. London: Arnold Publishing Ltd., 1984.

Articles

185.   Akinyemi, K. "A Study of Technophobia Among Primary School Teachers in Nigeria." *Programmed Learning and*

Educational Technology 23, No. 3 (1986): 263-69.

A study designed to investigate elementary teachers' apathy toward the use of equipment in instruction. Teachers involved in the study demonstrated a lack of knowledge of educational technology, but only slight traces of technophobia.

186. Nwagwu, Nicholas. "The Impact of Changing Conditions of Service on the Recruitment of Teachers in Nigeria." *Comparative Education* 17, No. 1 (1981): 81-86.

A survey taken in 1977 to determine if recent improvements in teaching conditions and benefits had affected high school graduates' attitudes toward primary teaching as a career.

187. Roberts, P.A. "Whose School?   Conflict Over School Management in Sefwi Wiawso, Ghana." *Anthropology and Education Quarterly* 13, No. 3 (1982): 268-78.

Examines the role of primary school teachers and community attitudes toward them. Problems are discussed which emerge as a result of conflicts between national institutions and community expectations.

188. Urwick, James. "Improving the Qualifications of Primary School Teachers in Nigeria: Official Goals and Practical Possibilities." *Compare* 17, No. 2 (1987): 137-55.

The rapid expansion of primary education has kept the number of untrained teachers at a substantial level. The author examines the causes and offers possible solutions.

Religion and Private Education

Books

189. Ojo, Gabriel A., ed. *The Church and the State in Education in Nigeria: Proceedings of the National Laity Council of Nigeria.* Ibadan: Marist Brothers of the Schools, 1981.

Reports on the Catholic Laity Council of Nigeria Conference and general meeting which took place in 1980.

Articles

190. Lemu, B. Aisha. "Islamization of Education: A Primary Level

of Experiment in Nigeria." *Muslim Education Quarterly* 5, No. 2 (1988): 76-80.

191.   Winter, Clyde A. "Koranic Education and Militant Islam in Nigeria." *International Review of Education* 33, No. 2 (1987): 171-86.

192.   Woodhouse, Howard R. "Moral and Religious Education for Nigeria." *Journal of Moral Education* 14, No. 2 (1985): 120-31.

Examines traditional education and its approach to moral education. Argues that moral and religious education are different and independent. The goals of moral education are discussed.

Education for Women

Books

*   Greenstreet, Miranda. *Females in the Agricultural Labour Force and Nonformal Education for Rural Development in Ghana*. Cited above as item 143.

193.   Ware, Helen, ed. *Women, Education and Modernization of the Family in West Africa*. Canberra: Australian National University Press, 1981.

A collection of works which focus on women and the family. The authors are drawn from a wide range of disciplines from sociology and anthropology to demography and comparative literature. It covers such countries as the Cameroun, Nigeria, Mali and Guinea. Chapter titles describe such topics as wage earner and mother, women and work, a study of female and male attitudes, traditional and modern family structures, and education and fertility. The book is carefully researched and makes good use of tables and figures. This is the seventh volume in a series begun in 1972. They came out of the changing African Family Project which is a collaborative project between the University of Ibadan and the Australian National University.

Articles

194.   Afemikhe, Ozame A. "Educational Plans and Aspirations of University Female Students in Nigeria." *Journal of Negro Education* 57, No. 4 (1988): 512-23.

195.   Csapo, Margaret. "Religious, Social and Economic Factors

Hindering the Education of Girls in Northern Nigeria."
Comparative Education 17, No. 3 (1981): 311-19.

Examines eight factors in Hausa Moslem society that tend to cause
parents to limit their daughter's education. Two of the factors are
marriage and the traditional women's role.

CENTRAL AFRICA

The central region of the African Continent is primarily composed of the former Belgian Congo, now Zaire, and the area once referred to as French Equatorial Africa -- Chad, Congo-Brazzaville and Gabon. Added to this is the coastal country of Cameroon and two small, but heavily populated countries in the Eastern section -- Burundi and Rwanda. It is an enormous territory that stretches from the equatorial rain forests of Zaire to the desert like conditions found in Chad. For the most part it is lightly populated and much of the interior is isolated with large sections lacking modern communication and transportation systems.

Since the 1960's the region has seen a great deal of political turmoil and ethnic rivalry. This often has led to armed conflict, involving coups and civil wars. Peaceful conditions often are brought about through the emergence of strong leaders who suppress ethnic divisions.

Central Africa's economic future appears to depend upon its mineral wealth and natural resources. To develop these resources countries have turned to concession companies, a practice begun and encouraged by the former colonial metropoles. The four nations that were former members of the Federation of Equatorial Africa joined with the state of Cameroon in a confederation to promote regional cooperation and economic development.

There is a paucity of literature written in the English language concerning the region's educational development. Prior to independence the former French colonies were often neglected except for some mission education that produced a few civil servants and a small group of educated elite found in urban areas. A few students in rural areas, who went to school, heard and spoke French while in the classroom, then went home to a different world of family and tradition. Islamic schools were found throughout the area, but the lack of concentrated population centers made it difficult for these schools to offer more than a rudimentary education.

The former Belgian Congo and the small countries of Burundi and Rwanda also were dominated by Christian missions. With few exceptions education was confined to elementary schooling in the vernacular and some post-primary vocational training. Schools did not offer a complete secondary education with the exception of the Roman Catholic seminaries that trained a select few for the priesthood. The rationale was that the majority of the people would continue to live in a rural and traditional society. When independence came it was estimated that, excluding priests, there were fewer than twenty Congolese who had graduated from four-year colleges. There was little opportunity for the kind of education found in other parts of the continent where some Africans had at least a limited opportunity for the type of education that helped prepare them to take an active role in the political and economic development of their country.

CAMEROON

Overview

Cameroon's unique colonial status continues to influence education in the country today. Each of the three colonial countries -- France, Germany and Great Britain -- left their language and educational philosophy as a legacy. The language problem is compounded in this nation of 12 million by well over 150 ethnolinguistic groups, at least a quarter of them of major importance. Today, the nation is officially bilingual -- French and English -- but with 80% of the population living in the French-speaking sector, the language dominates in the administration of the country and in the schools. As an oil-exporting nation, Cameroon has the necessary financial resources to undertake an ambitious plan of educational expansion. However, the rapid growth of educational opportunity has occurred primarily through mission schools that dominate primary and teacher education.

Structure

Educational management takes place through the six departments of the Ministry of National Education. They are assisted by inspectors of primary schools in each of the 40 administrative divisions and by national inspectors for subjects taught in the secondary schools. Private schools are expected to follow the same administrative and curriculum regulations as the public schools. Those approved by the government receive grants to pay teachers' salaries. The educational ladder differs in the English- and French-speaking areas. The Anglophone system consists of 7 years of primary schooling followed by 5 years of secondary and topped by 2 additional years leading to an external examination. The Francophone system includes 6 years of primary education followed by a 4-year plus 3-year lycée-styled secondary school. The two systems merge in higher education where students are expected to be bilingual. The University of Cameroon, founded in 1960, is officially bilingual, but administratively and culturally it is dominated by the French language.

Function

While the government is attempting to harmonize the two separate systems, the overall curriculum remains closely allied to the colonial pattern. The primary schools are expected to send the better students into classical secondary schools that stress the liberal arts and both languages. Despite the quantitative expansion of educational opportunity the drop out rate is very high. Only 10% of those who begin primary education receive a completion certificate. The shortage of qualified teachers and the language barriers tend to be cited as reasons for the high wastage rate. The government is attempting to build a national identity through the schools and to introduce practical rural and agricultural oriented courses through specially designed programs, but these efforts have met with little success. More successful is the government's rural based nonformal education program that stresses functional literacy for the adult population.

CENTRAL AFRICAN REPUBLIC

Overview

This land locked and sparsely populated country has endured a considerable amount of political turmoil since independence. The political instability coupled with a lack of finances is hindering the nation's educational development. The problem is further compounded by a rural-based population, many of whom are engaged in subsistence agriculture. In spite of these problems the government brought under its control all private schools and educational expansion is happening.

Structure and Function

The Ministry of National Education administers a predominantly French styled system of education. A 6-year primary school is followed by a 4-year junior secondary and 3-year senior secondary school. Examinations are administered at all levels. University admission requires the baccalaureate. A very small percentage of students reaches the nation's university. The government is attempting to diversify the curriculum in order to supply the necessary middle and high level trained personnel. A new educational policy requires students to choose a field of study in relation to the development plans established by the government. By the 1980's there were university institutes for mining and geology, and agricultural technology. The government is emphasizing nonformal education and through its efforts the literacy rate has increased to 40%.

CHAD

Overview

This lightly populated country has one of the world's lowest per capita incomes and highest illiteracy rates. Upon independence the new government inherited from the French only the semblance of an educational system with a school enrollment ratio one of the lowest in Francophone Africa. For the past two decades the country has been engaged in a civil war that has virtually closed the school system in the north and left little funds available in the southern part of the country.

Structure and Function

The Ministry of Education administers all education in the country which is divided into six educational regions headed by principal inspectors. The six regions are further divided into 18 divisions headed by inspectors. The school structure has changed little since independence. French is the language of instruction and the curriculum is dominated by the liberal arts. Recent efforts have been made to develop technical education at the secondary level. Almost 90% of the primary school children are enrolled in state schools. The Muslim north does contain some Koranic schools. Primary education lasts for 6 years and is followed by a secondary education composed of a first cycle of 4 years followed by a second cycle of 3 years. Progress through the system is slowed by a very selective examination system. The large majority of the students are male. Primary school enrollment is expanding dramatically in spite of a lack of trained teachers. The University of Chad was established in 1971 and is composed of four institutes, one of which is the Institute of Animal Husbandry. More Chadian students receive their higher education abroad than attend the University of Chad. Most go to French institutions.

PEOPLE'S REPUBLIC OF THE CONGO

Overview

This nation of two million people, situated astride the equator, has three distinctive features that separate it from its neighbors. The increased production of oil during the 1980's has placed the economy on a sound footing. Over 90% of its income from exports comes from this production. A second distinction can be found around the capital city of Brazzaville which served as the second administrative center, after Dakar, for the French colonial empire in Africa. This favored position left schools and an administrative structure in place when independence came in 1960.

The most distinctive feature is the movement of the government toward a Marxist-Leninist position. Initially referred to as "scientific socialism" a succession of "Marxist" rulers have maintained this ideology. However, recent political unrest leaves the future position of this ideology in doubt.

The political position has affected education. In 1965 all schools were nationalized and in 1980 a major reform established "people's schools." The main purpose of these schools is to develop a close association between schooling and productive work. The direction for this association is spelled out in the nation's 1982-86 five year plan. Yet, in spite of these reforms the overall school system maintains a strong French character.

Structure

The Ministry of National Education manages schooling through seven directorates housed within the Ministry and ten administrative regions. Education is compulsory for a 10-year basic period divided into a 6-year primary level and a 4-year second level. During the second level students choose between general education, including polytechnic education, and vocational education.

Well over 20% of the nation's budget is devoted to education. This funding has led to a spectacular rise in the schools' populations. Unfortunately the infrastructure has not kept pace nor has the preparation of qualified teachers. Many secondary schools lack laboratories and equipment of all kinds. In some urban areas schooling is held in shifts to meet demands. Overall the accomplishments are impressive. Equally impressive is the nation's commitment to eradicate illiteracy. The country has been awarded prizes on three different occasions for its programs from UNESCO during the international literacy campaigns.

Function

The curriculum has several special features. Attempts are being made to introduce Congolese languages, and regional variations in the overall curriculum are permitted. The emphasis on polytechnical and vocational education is partially a result of the nation's ideological stance. The move to associate education with productive work through skilled training is hindered by the lack of trained teachers in several areas. It also is handicapped by an inherent belief that the most prestigious education occurs in those schools that have maintained their tie to French tradition.

GABON

Overview

Gabon is a small nation of one million people who live in an area primarily covered by equatorial forests. One-half of the population is engaged in subsistence agriculture. Its rich deposits of manganese, and recently discovered oil, help to make it one of the richest countries in Sub-Saharan Africa. The availability of money has helped to produce an adult population that is 90% literate and has led to the quantitative expansion of educational opportunity. There is a resident European population in the country, mostly French, who are employed in various occupations including teaching.

Structure and Function

The Ministry of Education administers both public and private schools. Private religious-oriented schools enroll over 40% of all students through the secondary level. The private schools receive state aid and follow the national curriculum. Education is free for all students from primary school thorough the university. Unlike many parts of the continent, more females are enrolled in the schools than males. The educational ladder consists of a 6-year primary school followed by a secondary education that is divided into a 4-year junior and 2-year senior level. Students who enter the academic stream for the last 2 years are prepared for the university. The overall system closely parallels the French system with terminal examinations at each level. The National University of Libreville offers degree programs that are recognized in all of Francophone Africa and France.

A high rate of attrition remains a serious problem as does the difficulty of delivering educational services to rural areas where the transportation system is poor. Another pervasive problem is the propensity of students to seek an academic education even though opportunities in technical and vocational education lead directly to employment in the mining industry.

ZAIRE

Overview

The history of Zaire is often cited as an example of colonialism at its worst. The colony known as the Congo was originally the private fiefdom of the Belgian King Leopold II, who sold off large tracts of land to European companies. When the Belgian government took over the colony's administration they introduced the twin principles of paternalism and gradualism. In education this translated into primary basic education to meet laboring needs. There was little room for general education and no public secondary or higher education was permitted. When independence came to Zaire in 1960, few citizens had been prepared for positions of responsibility. The problem was magnified during the 1960's when civil war hindered educational development.

Another colonial feature that influences education today is the extent to which religious missions have maintained a monopoly on education. The monopoly began in 1906 when the Belgian government entered into an agreement with the Vatican. The agreement authorized Catholic missionaries to establish schools in return for government subsidies and large land concessions. Later Protestant missions were extended the same privilege. During the 1970's the independent government brought radical reform through a policy of nationalization. This included the missionary schools. However, by 1977 the system was near collapse and the government reversed itself and returned the schools to the missions.

Structure

The administration of education is influenced by its accommodation to the missions and the very rapid expansion of education. Deprived of real opportunity under colonialism the new citizens see education as an important symbol of independence. The spectacular expansion of education places a strain on what the government can supply. The problem is compounded by a large population growth that has seen the country grow from 14 million in 1960 to an estimated 36 million in 1990. There is every indication that the demand for education will continue to grow.

The Ministry of Primary and Secondary Education and the Ministry of Higher Education manage the system with assistance from departments in the provinces. Both the Catholic and Protestant bureaus of education are influential and operate as independent educational agencies.

The educational ladder consists of 6 years of primary education. In some rural areas this is divided between 2 years lower primary and 4 years upper primary grades. Secondary education offers several options and is quite complex. All students who enter secondary education begin with a 2-year cycle, which emphasizes the French language, the sciences and mathematics. This is followed by either a short-cycle school that provides 2-3 terminal technical programs or long-cycle schools that offer four categories of an academic 4-year program. Educational mobility is controlled by a series of examinations. The examination system and the academic nature of the early curriculum are two reasons why the system is greatly imbalanced. Over 90% of all students are enrolled in primary education and many of these in the first two years.

The government's attempt to nationalize the three universities in the 1970's collapsed. However, the three independent institutions, for the most part, have maintained their areas of academic specialization developed during the nationalized period. One of the three universities is public and the other two are private and were established by the Catholic and Protestant missionaries.

Function

When independence came, the movement was toward an academic curriculum and away from the colonial imposed vocational training. As a consequence the vocational and technical schools receive little support. Educational parity among the newly developing academic oriented secondary schools appears to become more important as does parity with the Belgian system. The higher education curriculum is a replica of the Belgian universities. Some movement is being made to Africanize the curriculum and to adapt primary education to local conditions. Religious education is still important. Attempts to reintroduce indigenous languages at the primary level is meeting some success, but the language of instruction at the secondary and higher level is French.

The shortage of classrooms and qualified teachers is a common problem in many parts of the developing world. However the problem is compounded in Zaire by a huge population growth, a drift toward urban centers and a national government without a clear plan for educational development.

BIBLIOGRAPHY

Cameron, John, ed. *International Handbook of Educational Systems*: Volume II. Chichester: John Wiley and Sons, 1983.

deLusignan, Guy. *French Speaking Africa Since Independence.*

New York: Frederick A. Praeger, 1969.

Fafunwa, A. Babs and J. U. Aisiku, eds. *Education in Africa: A Comparative Survey*. London: George Allen and Unwin, 1982.

Faraj, Abdulatif Hussein. *International Yearbook of Education*, Volume XL-1988. Paris:UNESCO, 1988.

George, Betty. *Educational Development in the Congo*. Washington, D.C.: U.S. Government Printing Office, 1966.

Husen, Torsten and T. Postlethwaite, eds. *The International Encyclopedia of Education*. Oxford: Pergamon Press Ltd., 1985.

Kurian, George T., ed. *World Education Encyclopedia*. New York: Facts on File Publications, 1988.

Mukweso, Mwenene, George Papagiannis and Sande Milton. "Education and Occupational Attainment from Generation to Generation: The Case of Zaire," in *Comparative Education Review*, Vol. 28, No. 1, February, 1984.

World Bank. *Education in Sub-Saharan Africa*. Washington, D.C.: The World Bank, 1988.

ANNOTATED BIBLIOGRAPHY

History and Philosophy

Books

196.   Mbuagbaw, Tanyi. *African Philosophy of Education*. Yaounde: SOPECAM, 1984.

The author is from the Cameroon and bases the philosophical look at education on Cameroonian culture. The problems faced by the schools in that country are confronted through an African perspective based on local tradition.

Education and Development

Books

197.   Chinapah, Vinayagum. *Swedish Missions and Education in the Republic of Zaire: A Description and Diagnosis*. Stockholm: Institute of International Education, University of Stockholm, 1981.

Articles

198.   Mukweso, Mwenene and Others. "Education and Occupational Attainment from Generation to Generation: The Case of Zaire." *Comparative Education Review* 28, No. 1 (1984): 52-68.

A study to determine the relationship between education and occupation. It uses specific Zaire historical and cultural factors. Variables were socioeconomic background, tribe, religion, urban experience, type of school, educational attainment, job experience and occupational attainment. The sample includes people who matured in preindependence and postindependence periods.

Secondary Education

Books

199.   Bafoua, Justin. *An Examination of Indiscipline in Secondary Schools in the Congo*.   Nairobi: African Curriculum Organization Project, 1983.

Tertiary and Higher Education

Books

200. Anicet, Mawaka. *An Examination of the Structure and Organisation of Teaching Practice in Primary Teachers Training Colleges in the People's Republic of the Congo.* Nairobi: African Curriculum Organization Project, 1982.

Specialized Education (Adult, Community, Nonformal, Technical, Vocational)

Books

201. Fitzgerald, E.P., ed. "Vocational and Technical Education in French Equatorial Africa, 1842-1960." *Proceedings of the Eighth Annual Meeting of the French Colonial Historical Society, 1982.* Lanham, MD: University Press of America, 1985.

202. Ngoma, Jean Jeannot. *The Impact of Rural Adult Education on Socioeconomic Development in the Congo.* Nairobi: African Curriculum Organization Project, 1983.

203. Wakatama, M.A. *Correspondence Education in Central Africa: An Alternative Route to Higher Education in Developing Countries.* Lanham, MD: University Press of America, 1983.

Curriculum and Methods

Books

204. Mombod, Josephine Ntinou. *Developing Models/Techniques in the Teaching of English as a Second Foreign Language in Senior Secondary Schools in the Congo.* Nairobi: African Curriculum Organization Project, 1983.

Articles

205. Bryant, Daniel. "Teaching Physics in Cameroon." *Physics Teacher* 21, No. 1 (1983): 12-16.

Describes the American author's experiences teaching high school physics. Comments on the educational system, instructional strategies, material, equipment and personal experiences.

Teachers

Books

206.   Kouma, Felix. *A Study of Problems Faced by Teachers in the Congo and Some Practical Solutions.* Nairobi: African Curriculum Organization Project, 1981.

207.   Luma, Lydia Eveny'a. *The Education of African Teachers.* Yaounde, Cameroon: SOPECAM, 1983.

Religion and Private Education

Articles

208.   MacGaffey, Wyatt. "Education, Religion, and Social Structure in Zaire." *Anthropology and Education Quarterly* 13, No. 3 (1982): 238-50.

Analyzes the relations between indigenous and western education during the transformation from precolonial times to the present. Explores the relationships between education, religion, social structure and social stratification patterns.

209.   Sheline, Yvonne E. and Others. "The Effect of School Sponsorship on Academic Achievement: A Comparison of Catholic, Protestant and Government Secondary Schools in Zaire." *Comparative Education* 20, No. 2 (1984): 223-36.

Suggests that school sponsorship serves as an indicator of future social power and that the perception of social power motivates students. Describes the charter system, compares the sponsors, reviews education since 1908 and cites implications for educational policy.

Education for Women

Articles

210.   Dwight, Margaret L. "Cameroonian Women at the Crossroads: Their Changing Roles and Status." *Journal of African Studies* 13, No. 4 (1986-87): 126-30.

EAST AFRICA

Current educational patterns in East Africa have been greatly affected by three major factors, two of which occurred during the colonial period. The first was the domination by Great Britain during the colonial era. The second was European settlement and "hands-on" administration during the same period, and thirdly, the divergent political and economic paths taken after independence.

Cecil Rhodes' dream of British domination from "the Cape to Cairo" was manifested in East Africa. The partition of Africa by European powers led to the establishment of the British East Africa Protectorate in 1895. When Germany was forced to surrender Tanganyika after its defeat in World War I, Britain's sphere of influence extended through Tanganyika, Kenya, Uganda, British Somaliland, and the Sudan.

The pattern of intervention was similar throughout the area. The Christian missionaries came first, often supported financially by British trading companies. They were followed by the Imperial British East Africa Company interested in commercial enterprises. The Company soon demanded protection from the British government. Unlike West Africa, where the British ruled through indigenous chiefs, the British colonial government began to directly intervene in the administration of its colonies. The "hands-on" administration policy took a new turn when European settlement began in earnest in the Kenya Colony after World War I.

The British government encouraged white settlement in the belief that the highlands were a rich and unexploited land that could produce the raw materials needed for British industrial development. What European settlement brought was the uneasy confrontation between two alien cultures that led to the privilege of race and status supported by a colonial administration. For the Africans it meant land exploitation, segregated communities and education, inferior status in their own land, forced labor policies and forced taxation.

However, European settlement also brought the semblance of a political and communication infra-structure, a wage-earning economy, large scale agricultural development and an expanded system of education primarily through the encouragement of missionary schools. The initial role of the mission schools to "Christianize and Civilize" the indigenous people was expanded in order to meet the European demand for clerical and commercial employees as well as low-level bureaucratic jobs in the colonial administration.

In some areas the people resisted European penetration and the economic and educational influences that came with it. However, other people responded favorably, sometimes in order to better understand the people who were now controlling their lives. Regional differences in educational opportunity became apparent. More schools were developed in those areas where receptivity was best and in urban areas that appeared in order to cater to European settlers and administrators. The proximity of the European to the African on a day-to-day basis soon became proof that an academic-styled education brought more prestige and more money. Access to white collar jobs was through academic institutions, not through schools established to promote vocational training. When independence came to the region the colonial heritage had left regional inequities and the emergence of a small urban based educated elite who favored a British style literary education.

In spite of strong British colonial influence throughout the area, with independence other strong social, political, and economic forces began to emerge. These forces dramatically influenced contemporary educational practices in several ways. In the Sudan open conflict between the Islamic north and Christian influence in the south represented basic differences between the two religious faiths in the Arab and Western worlds. The religious problems faced there are being observed by African leaders in the Western and Central parts of the continent where several countries share an uneasy truce between the two doxologies.

In Somalia similar religious and educational problems exist, but this issue appears minor in a nation where in the worst of times continuous warfare between clans make a mockery of nationhood; and where in the best of times the language of instruction in schools could be Arabic, Somali, English, or Italian, the language of the former colonizer. An example would be the national university where the language of instruction is Italian, except in the College of Education where English is used.

In the past, Somalia also shared a political force with several African countries that greatly influenced the schools. That force was socialism. Sometimes it was a special type of African socialism, other times it was the Marxist-Leninist style. In recent days this political form influenced Ethiopia and in days just past it was a pervasive influence in Tanzania. The neighboring countries of Tanzania and Kenya are often contrasted because of their socio-political policies that affect their economic direction and their schools.

With independence, Kenya opted for a capitalist economy. The new nation openly sought aid and investors from the West and attempted to build an industrial base to complement its agricultural development. In education the government expanded educational opportunity by encouraging both public and private schools. While the curriculum has been Africanized in some areas, the British academic orientation has been maintained and English has become the preferred language of instruction. One result is that the cognitive skill level of the average employee has risen and the urban areas have seen the emergence of an educated elite that have, in part, moved beyond their ethnic identity. Other results include a growing number of secondary school leavers and graduates who are unemployed and do not want to return to their rural homes, large regional inequities, both economically and educationally, and a growing economic disparity between rural and urban areas.

In contrast, Tanzania after independence opted for a socialist model of government and promoted education for self-reliance. Under the leadership of their visionary President, Julius Nyerere, the nation turned away from the West and opted to develop itself from within. This meant agricultural development including the establishment of large communes and government control of commerce and industry. In education this meant an emphasis on practical rural-oriented education for the vast majority of the youth and close government supervision of the schools. Primary education was to be terminal for most students, the language of instruction was Swahili and the emphasis was on the teaching of agricultural and vocational skills for rural development. Graduates were expected to stay in their rural communities. Only a few students had the opportunity to go on to secondary education where English was the medium of instruction, but the emphasis was away from the development of academic skills. The majority of the graduates were expected to return to the rural areas and assist in development activities.

By 1980 divergent educational policies in Tanzania and Kenya had led to secondary enrollment ratios that showed six times more students enrolled in Kenya than in Tanzania. However, Tanzania's policy of self-reliance and rural development has furnished primary education for all, greatly reduced the illiteracy rate, and provided access to rural health dispensaries and safe drinking water for the majority.

Unfortunately Tanzania's costly war with Uganda, rising oil prices, low prices for their agricultural products and poor management by the government has brought the country to the brink of bankruptcy. As Tanzania enters the decade of the 90's it appears that much of the experimentation with socialism is behind them. The nation has a new president and is moving toward a free market economy. A new educational policy has encouraged the development of private and public secondary schools. More English is now being used in the schools and a restructuring of the curriculum has begun in order to supply middle and high level manpower needs for economic reasons.

Tanzania in particular, and East Africa as a whole, has shown the resilience of the peoples' demand for more educational opportunity. For the majority it is the only avenue that leads to full participation in the modern wage earning sector of the economy.

ETHIOPIA

Overview

Ethiopia is a unique country on the world scene. Not only is it one of the oldest nations in the world, but until World War II it enjoyed one of the longest periods of independence. Its isolated position in the middle of mountainous terrain helped to ensure this independence. From the fourth century the Christian Ethiopian Orthodox Church dominated the country culturally and educationally. The leaders of the church were treated as a privileged elite who were not only educators, but also held political power. Much later the Moslems and Ethiopian Jews, both minority groups, also provided religious oriented schools.

During the present century some attempts were made to develop a public school system. A Ministry of Education was established and, when the Italian occupation ended with World War II, the Emperor, Haile Selassie, decreed that part of the taxes collected by the central church treasury be allocated to promote public education. Because of British assistance and influence, English became an important language in the public schools. During this period some American influence also was evident as American advisors and classroom material were utilized. Attempts to modernize the system took an abrupt turn in 1974 when a revolution occurred. The new leaders dethroned Haile Selassie, dissolved parliament, and introduced a socialist government.

The first major action of the new government was to send teachers and students from the secondary schools and colleges out to the rural areas for one year to teach literacy and to build schools, roads and health facilities. The goal was to eradicate illiteracy by the end of the 80's. In 1975 another proclamation nationalized all primary and lower secondary schools, except mission schools, and placed their management in the hands of peasant and urban dwellers' associations. Additional government decrees provided policy guidelines for educational development that included free education for the masses, the establishment of a body to ensure that the school curriculum was formulated on the basis of Marxism-Leninism and priority placement on the development of science and technology courses. Clearly this nation of over 40 million people, 90% of whom lived in rural areas, was on a new road toward educational development. Unfortunately sustaining that road was difficult in the 80's primarily because of war and drought conditions. The 90's bring a new government and a new orientation. It is difficult to foresee what the future holds.

Structure and Function

The Socialist government, through its Ministry of Education, set ambitious goals for education. It is being assisted through the mobilization of large citizens' groups to assist in the building and management of the schools. One target for the mid-1990's is universal polytechnic education through grade 8. Another goal is to expand educational opportunity. The government's progress in this area is impressive, but a shortage of teachers is producing an extremely high teacher-pupil ratio.

The government also wants education more closely related to productive work, especially in rural areas. This means a shift in the curriculum toward a socialist respect for labor and skill development in such areas as agricultural techniques, irrigation, house and road construction and reforestation. The shift toward mass education and literacy means less money for the development of higher education. Some consolidation and reorganization of the university system is taking place and more students are receiving scholarships to study in Eastern Europe and the Soviet Union. It is difficult to determine whether this will continue.

The boldness of the educational reform has helped to bring external aid from international organizations such as UNESCO, the European Economic Community and the World Bank. Whether the reforms will be successful might depend on rain, armed struggle both within and outside the country's boundaries and the fragility of the political system.

KENYA

Overview

Kenya is often used as an example of an African nation that has not stood still since independence. Blending its colonial past with an African perspective, the government has attempted to modernize its economy and raise the standard of living of its people. This has been done by advocating free enterprise, promoting the development of tourism and industry to complement its agricultural development and encouraging foreign investment.

Unfortunately much of its economic progress has been blunted by the highest population growth rate in the world. This demographic trend has serious implications for education. In spite of a continuous increase in school enrollments at all levels, expansion has not been able to keep pace with demand. Although the government has allocated more money to education than any other social service, the future ability to provide educational opportunity for a greater percentage of the youth is in doubt.

Structure

The structure of education has been consistently changing over the past two decades as the government searches for ways to help make education more efficient and effective, and to link it more closely to economic development. In 1986 there was another reorganization of the ministry. Now called the Ministry of Education, Science and Technology, it administers a centralized system through seven administrative provinces which are divided further into districts and divisions. The central ministry is assisted by the Department of Adult Education housed in the Ministry of Culture and Social Services. The Department is responsible for the creation of learning opportunities for adults, the promotion of ethnic languages and the use of Swahili as a national language.

Primary education is universal and free. Its length was recently increased from seven to eight years. Admission into the four-year government-funded secondary schools requires students to successfully pass the Certificate of Primary Education examination. Recently the government reformed the examination because of criticism that it rewarded memorization and discouraged curriculum reform and imaginative teaching.

At the secondary level the government has permitted local communities to develop their own schools. The self-help "Harambee" schools now outnumber government aided schools. Although they differ widely in their quality and the ability of their students, they represent community efforts to provide educational opportunity for their youth. Many communities also have developed local polytechnic schools that offer specific skills and trades that often can be used in the local area. The government also has developed secondary technical schools and its own polytechnics, usually at a more advanced level than those of local communities.

Opportunities for a university education have greatly expanded in the past two decades. The government finances most of the recurring costs, but students are now given loans to cover their accommodations and other living expenses. They are expected to pay back the loans when they are employed. The traditional four-year university education is being supplemented with the establishment of institutes for such specific studies as African Affairs, Population and Research, Development Education and Adult Education. Recently the government opened a new university with a technological orientation. Comparatively large numbers of Kenyans receive their higher education in Great Britain and the United States.

Function

Curriculum development at the primary level is being assisted by the preparation of materials through the Institute of Education and by their publication in Kenya through a government-sponsored foundation. This ensures the addition of an African perspective to classroom material. Teachers' Centers attached to teacher training colleges also assist in this effort. Interactive educational radio is being used successfully to involve school children as active participants in the teaching of language. In rural schools the language of instruction is either the local vernacular or Swahili, followed by English from the third year onward. In urban areas, and increasingly in rural areas, schools begin with English language instruction from the first day of school. Both at the secondary and higher education level English is used.

Secondary schools continue to offer primarily an academic styled education. An African Social Studies Program is affecting the curriculum and a greater emphasis recently is being placed on the sciences and mathematics. Students attending government secondary schools tend to do better in the sciences. Few "Harambee" schools have laboratories or qualified science teachers. Entrance into higher education is through a competitive examination.

Large-scale expansion at all levels of education is creating a shortage of qualified teachers as well as school buildings and supplies. Still, Kenya's large investment in education is helping to increase the productivity of its work force and for a small number of educated elite a substantially higher standard of living. Whether the investment will continue to pay in the future could depend, in part, on the nation's population growth rate.

SOMALIA

Overview

Somalia is a poor country with land that ranges from semi-arid to arid desert. Well over half the people are nomadic herders who follow their sheep and camels. Since independence in 1960 there has been almost continuous armed struggle between the various clans as well as war with neighboring Ethiopia. Prior to independence the country was divided into two colonies -- British Somaliland in the north and Italian Somaliland in the south. Both colonies attempted to introduce formal education. In the Italian sector the language of instruction was Italian for all schooling. In the British sector Arabic was used for the first three years followed by English. Often formal education was introduced through Christian missionaries who saw their efforts thwarted by the dominant Moslem population. Differences between the two colonists and the Islamic religious orientation continued to affect educational development after independence.

Structure and Function

The educational system is based on a series of presidential decrees rather than legislative action. After independence the new government established a Ministry of Education and attempted to unify the Italian and British systems. In 1970, the country was declared a socialist state by the new president and throughout that decade education assumed a new structure and a sense of direction. Most private education, primarily provided by Roman Catholic missions, was nationalized and a Somali-oriented curriculum was introduced. Koranic schools operate along side the government system although their number is not large. In 1972, the Somali language was put into written form and an official Latin script adopted. A government printing plant began to produce materials in the new written language. By 1975 primary education was 8 years in duration and the number of youth enrolled greatly expanded. It was followed by a 4-year secondary school. During the 70's the number of secondary schools also was expanded and spread throughout the country. Secondary education terminated with an examination, the results determining who went on to the Somali National University.

It is difficult to say what the future holds for formal education. Continuous warfare is depriving the system of money and stability.

Whether the people could unite under one strong leader is difficult to determine. Their common language could help to build unity; so could a unified school system.

THE SUDAN

Overview

This former British colony is the largest country in size on the African continent. It often has been described as the nation that bridges Arab and Black Africa. In the north desert-like land, the Arabic language, and the Islamic religion provide a unifying influence, while in the south there is a plethora of ethnic languages and customs. Altogether there are over 500 identifiable clans in the Sudan divided into over 50 ethnic groups. The diversity within the country and between the north and south have major implications for education.

Also influencing educational development has been a series of civil wars since independence, most often between the north and south. The results have led to more regional autonomy, but they also have caused serious political and economic problems. The Sudan has been ranked by the World Bank as one of the world's poorest countries based on its gross national product.

Structure

With independence the new government inherited the semblance of a British system of education, but in reality there were three systems: the Koranic schools in the north, the Christian mission schools in the rural south and the government schools found primarily in urban areas. Throughout the colonial administration English became the language of instruction in the schools.

Until 1980 all education was centralized and administered by the Ministry of Education and Guidance. However, in that year some regional autonomy was given that resulted in primary and intermediate schools being locally administered throughout the six regions. Each region is further divided into provinces and managed by assistant commissioners of education and school inspectors. The central ministry still maintains jurisdiction over secondary and higher education as well as the overall curriculum.

The educational ladder consists of a 6-year primary cycle which could begin and often end in a rural village school or a Koranic school. A regional examination is given at the end of 6 years to determine who goes on to a 3-year intermediate school with an academic orientation or a 2-year vocational youth center. Those who successfully pass the intermediate leaving examination move on to a 3-year academic secondary school or a 4-year technical school. The ladder is topped by universities and higher technical institutes. Over half the students enrolled in higher education are students at the University of Cairo, Khartoum branch, which basically offers an Egyptian-styled education.

Function

The majority of the students do not go beyond the primary school and, in spite of the government's efforts to "democratize" educational opportunity, a much larger percentage of students complete primary school in the north than in the south. The democratization process is succeeding in bringing more women into formal education. The overall numbers enrolled are increasing dramatically.

The primary school curriculum wrestles with the language problem. Some schools use English or Arabic as the language of instruction while others use the local vernacular. The curriculum at both the primary and secondary level attempts to link schooling with productive work, but the development of technical and vocational education lags behind the academic emphasis.

To confront the nation's high illiteracy rate and the lack of educational opportunity in rural areas, a plan has been developed to create Integrated Rural Education centers that will provide primary education for the youth and adults in basic and functional literacy. The development of these centers will be an important step toward linking education more closely to productive work.

TANZANIA

Overview

Tanzania is a nation of 22 million people in transition. The movement is away from a socialist state that attempted to reduce dependency on the international economic market. The new direction is toward a free market economy that gives incentives to individual farmers and dismantles some of the state's corporations. This shift has serious consequences for education. Under socialism "education for self-reliance" was designed to prepare young people for the work they would be called upon to perform in a rural society -- agriculture and village development. This meant an emphasis on skills that would promote agricultural production and marketing, and an attitude that would foster the social goals of living and working together for a common good. Primary education was to be terminal with only 4 out of every 100 gaining admission to secondary schools and only 1 out of every 100, who began primary school, gaining admission to higher education.

Under a new president the socialist model has been modified and free enterprise is beginning to evolve. In education this means the continuing development of private secondary schools, for the most part promoted by local communities. The government also is expected to expand opportunities at all levels. A recent National Commissions' Report calls for not less than 15% of children completing primary education to enter government secondary schools by the year 2000. The same report calls for a clearly defined government action plan to promote scientific and technological education. Higher education is to expand to satisfy high-level manpower needs. Whether the nation's new leadership can move toward these goals is difficult to predict, especially with limited funds and some resistance from political and educational leaders who feel that the road to African socialism is the correct one for Tanzania.

Structure

The Ministry of National Education coordinates all formal and nonformal education for children and adults. It is assisted by an Institute of Education, involved in curriculum and material development, and an Institute of Adult Education that manages literacy and group campaigns to bring opportunities to rural areas. The Ministry administers through regional, district, division and ward level officers.

The educational ladder consists of a 7-year primary school, 4 years of lower secondary school, and a 2-year additional academic program for the few who go on to higher education. The University of Dar es Salaam was established in 1970 and is the nation's highest center of learning. A faculty of agriculture with its own college is located in Morogoro, a rural area. Post-primary craft centers offer 2 year programs designed to develop schools for rural development and four secondary technical schools help to provide mid-level skilled personnel.

Function

The introduction of universal and free primary education in the 70's has led to rapid expansion at this level. An emphasis is placed on the development of school farms as an integral part of the curriculum. Also included in the curriculum are practical skills needed to develop rural communities. In theory local farmers and community leaders are suppose to help the primary school teacher who often has the responsibility for adult education in the community. Swahili is the language of instruction. It is spoken throughout the country and is a unifying factor. Both primary and secondary schools are expected to move toward becoming economically self-supporting. This means that the school farms must produce enough food to feed the students and to sell the surplus for school income. Secondary schools are attempting to diversify their curriculum and vocationalize. Each secondary school is expected to introduce at least one of four practical and work-oriented subjects -- agricultural science, domestic science, a commercial course, or a technical course. English is the language of instruction.

Prior to the new reform movement students were expected to spend at least one year working in a productive capacity before being admitted to higher education. The new reform suggests that students go directly to higher education from secondary schools. The need to supply high-level skilled personnel is necessary for economic development. The reform also places renewed emphasis on English language teaching and usage in order to provide a window to the world for business and commercial leaders. How far that window should open or will open is still being discussed by the new leadership.

UGANDA

Overview

When this nation in the heart of Africa received its independence from Great Britain in 1962 the future looked bright. Fertile land had produced an agrarian based economy where only 30% of the rural inhabitants were engaged in subsistence agriculture. In education the country was further developed than any of its neighbors with Makerere, the only university college in Eastern Africa, sitting on the top of the pyramid, and the infra-structure of a colonial system beneath it.

Unfortunately this situation changed dramatically when a "total national calamity" began with a 1971 coup that brought self-appointed General Idi Amin to political power. After eight years of his regime a liberating force of Tanzanian soldiers and Ugandans overthrew Amin. What followed was a succession of governments that attempted to restore the previous stability in the face of civil unrest and armed conflict between rival groups. It has been only in the last few years that national attention has been turned to education. What the new leaders found was the non-existence of financial resources, schools either destroyed or deteriorated and qualified teachers emigrated to other countries. Despite these problems a new educational course is being plotted and Uganda appears to be on the road to recovery.

Structure and Function

During the 1980's the government made efforts toward the rehabilitation of the educational infra-structure and developed plans for its recovery and advancement. The Recovery Program 1982/84 plan gave direction to education as did the country's Ten Year Development Plan, 1981-1990. Major policy orientations include the decentralization of educational administration, planning, and supervision and the encouragement of partnerships at the local level. The partnerships ask local communities to provide labor and money to refurbish schools while the government assists with the finances and the employment of teachers. The planning also calls for an emphasis on the development of day secondary schools rather than boarding schools, and an upgrading of teacher education.

A review of the curriculum has not been neglected during this period of recovery. The Uganda Commission for UNESCO recommends diversifying the curriculum by complementing the academic program with training in needed skills and placing emphasis on practical and immediately productive programs. One emphasis is on the value of self-reliance efforts through the development of school feeding projects. The nation's new leaders recognize that it will take awhile before the return of a modern wage earning sector that can hire well-educated people. The majority of recent graduates from Makerere University are jobless.

Uganda's educational recovery is beginning. It is assisted by local community efforts, the national government and international organizations. School enrollment at all levels continues to climb. Given a period of political and civil stability the nation could, once again, assume a position of educational leadership throughout the area.

BIBLIOGRAPHY

Bagunywa, Arthur M.K. *Critical Issues in African Education: A Case Study of Uganda*. Nairobi: East Africa Publishing House, 1980.

Cameron, John, ed. *International Handbook of Educational Systems*, Volume II. Chichester: John Wiley and Sons, 1983.

Eshiwani, George S. *Implementing Educational Policies in Kenya*. Washington, D.C.: The World Bank, 1990.

Fafunwa, A. Babs and J.U. Aisiku, eds. *Education in Africa: A Comparative Survey*. London: George Allen and Unwin, 1982.

Faraj, Abdulatif Hussein. *International Yearbook of Education, Volume XL-1988*. Paris: UNESCO, 1988.

Hawes, Hugh. *Curriculum and Reality in African Primary Schools*. Burnt Mill: Longman Group Ltd., 1979.

Hinzen, H. and V.H. Hundsdorfer, eds. *Education for Liberation and Development: The Tanzanian Experience*. Hamburg: UNESCO Institute for Education, 1982.

Husen, Torsten and T. Neville Postlethwaite, eds. *The International Encyclopedia of Education*. Oxford: Pergamon Press Ltd., 1985.

Kurian, George T., ed. *World Education Encyclopedia*. New York: Facts on File Publications, 1988.

Nkinyangi, John A. "Access to Primary Education in Kenya: The Contradictions of Public Policy," in *Comparative Education Review*, Vol. 26, No. 2, June, 1982.

Urch, George E. "The Role of Education in Restructuring Socialism: The Tanzanian Case," in *Educational Studies*, Vol. 15, No. 3, 1989.

World Bank. *Education in Sub-Saharan Africa*. Washington, D.C.: The World Bank, 1988.

ANNOTATED BIBLIOGRAPHY

History and Philosophy

Books

211. Anderson, John. *The Struggle for the School.* Nairobi: Longman Group Ltd., 1970.

Describes the interaction of missionaries, colonial government officials and nationalists in the evolution of formal education in Kenya. Much of the book is devoted to the pre-independence period. It is carefully documented. The author taught in Kenya during the 60's.

212. Cameron, J. and W. A. Dodd. *Society, Schools and Programs in Tanzania.* Oxford: Pergamon Press Ltd., 1970.

One in a series of "comparative" studies under the general editorship of Edmund King. Basically details the historical development of the formal system with periodic government reports serving as guidelines. The three major sections are entitled, "The Foundations," "The Road to Independence" and "Independence and After." Some attempt at analysis is made.

213. Furley, O. W. and T. Watson. *A History of Education in East Africa.* New York: NOK Publishers, 1978.

Contains a broad survey of educational history beginning with indigenous education and culminating with several chapters on the development of education since independence. The development of formal schools for each of the races is traced and the influences of both the British and German colonialists is discussed. The book pays special attention to the extent and type of educational expansion. Also considered is the impact of external pressures from the missionaries, through the colonial period to the United Nations.

214. Lawuo, Z. E. *Education and Social Change in a Rural Community.* Dar es Salaam: University Press, 1980.

Examines the way in which a rural community accepted Western formal education and used it to enhance its own development under colonial rule. It is a study of colonial education and local response among the Chagga in Tanzania between 1920 and 1945. It carefully documents specific ways in which self-help educational activities developed.

215.   Mbilinyi, M. *Who Goes to School in East Africa?* Dar es Salaam: Institute of Education, 1976.

216.   Meena, E. A. K. *Some Aspects of Education in Tanzania.* Dar es Salamm: Longman Tanzania, 1983.

217.   Sanderson, Lilian Passmore and Neville Sanderson. *Education, Religion and Politics in Southern Sudan, 1889-1964.* London: Ithaca Press, 1981.

Emanates from doctoral thesis research by Lilian Passmore Sanderson, supplemented by Neville Sanderson's studies on the administrative and "tribal" history of Southern Sudan. It is very detailed and carefully documented. The first half of the book focuses on missionary education, the second half on the relationship between the colonial government, local leaders and education.

218.   Sheffield, James R. *Education in Kenya: A Historical Study.* New York: Teachers College Press, 1973.

Traces the role of education from traditional society, through the colonial period to the post-independence period. Places education within the framework of the society at large. Good bibliography. One of a series published by the Center for Education in Africa, Teachers College.

219.   Wagaw, Teshome G. *Education in Ethiopia: Prospect and Retrospect.* Ann Arbor: University of Michigan Press, 1979.

Reported to be the first book on Ethiopian education authored by an Ethiopian. Analyzes the historical development of education from the early Christian era to the date of publication. Each chapter is devoted to a particular historical period within which the author deals with the major social and political issues that affected educational development. A special emphasis is given to the Ethiopian Orthodox Church, which historically assumed the responsibility of educating children and adults.

220.   Wandira, Asavia. *Early Missionary Education in Uganda.* Kampala: Makerere University, 1972.

The book was researched while the author was studying at the University of London. It describes how missionary education began and the goals it pursued. Also discussed are attempts made by missionary groups to adapt their education to the needs of society. The author's analysis is from a Ugandan perspective.

Articles

221. Bogonko, Sorobea N. "Aims of Eduction in Kenya Considered in the Context of Independence." *Kenya Journal of Education* 3, No. 1 (1986): 112-137.

Defines aims as production of manpower, individual development, liberation, cultural development and regeneration. Sees individual fulfillment as the key to all educational aims. Discusses the reforms implemented between 1963-1986 and reviews them in light of the colonial experience.

222. D'Souza, Henry. "Kenyan School and Culture." *Journal of Thought* 15, No. 2 (1980): 69-76.

Assesses African culture within a Kenyan context. Charts the culture from traditional thought through a national to an international focus. Suggests ways in which the schools can promote an international cultural standard.

223. Kassam, Yuusuf. "Nyerere's Philosophy and the Educational Experiment in Tanzania." *Interchange on Educational Policy* 14, No. 1 (1983): 56-68.

Examines the educational philosophy of Nyerere through his publications and reports on the major educational changes and reforms that have taken place.

Education and Development

Books

224. Auger, G.A., ed. *Tanzania Education since Uhuru: A Bibliography, 1961-1971.* Nairobi: East African Academy, 1973.

225. Bagunywa, Athur M.K. *Critical Issues in African Education: A Case Study of Uganda.* Nairobi: East African Publishing House, 1980.

226. Cameron, John. *The Development of Education in East Africa.* New York: Teachers College Press, 1970.

One in a series of books published by Teachers College Center for Education in Africa. The author was a member of the series editorial board. The book attempts to show how social, political and economic conditions in Kenya, Tanzania and Uganda affected the development and direction of education. A special emphasis is placed on teacher education.

227.   Court, David and Dharam P. Ghai, eds. *Education, Society and Development: New Perspectives from Kenya*. Nairobi: Oxford University Press, 1974.

Provides a series of articles that analyze educational concerns during the years after independence in Kenya. The articles focus on the relationship between the form and stage of Kenya's development on one hand and the nature of its educational system on the other. Most of the chapters are analytical and challenge the status quo.

228.   Eshiwani, George A.S. *Research in Eduction: The Kenya Register 1963-1980*. Nairobi: Bureau of Educational Research, Kenyatta University College, 1982.

229.   Evans, David R. *Teachers as Agents of National Development: A Case Study of Uganda*. New York: Praeger Publishers, 1971.

Analyzes teachers' attitudes and behavior along dimensions related to the national development goals of Uganda. The analysis of attitudes is set within the framework of ideas which are part of the process of political socialization. The teachers involved in the study represent a national sample from government secondary schools.

230.   Gumbel, P., K. Nystrom and R. Samuelsson. *Education in Ethiopia, 1974-82*. Stockholm: Swedish International Development Authority, 1983.

Developed by the Education Division of the Swedish International Development Authority. Offers a frank appraisal of what has been achieved through programs funded by Sweden.

231.   Kasozi, A.B.K. *The Crisis of Secondary School Education in Uganda, 1960-1970*. Kampala: Longman Uganda Ltd., 1979.

Highlights the problems associated with the rapid expansion of secondary schools after independence. The problems include the undermining of traditional values, little association between the type of secondary education received and employment opportunities and financial difficulties. One chapter is a case study of a "typical Ugandan secondary school in 1968." The author offers some possible solutions to the problems.

232.   Keller, Edmond J. *Education, Manpower and Development:*

The Impact of Educational Policy in Kenya. Nairobi: Kenya Literature Bureau, 1980.

233. Kurtz, Laura A. *An African Education: The Social Revolution in Tanzania.* Brooklyn: Pageant-Poseidon Ltd., 1972.

Based on dissertation research, the study analyzes the implications which surround the development of educational policy in post-independent Tanzania. Special emphasis is placed on Nyerere's writings. Chapters also discuss the historical influence of the German and British colonial educators.

234. McKinley, Juanita E., ed. *Education in Kenya: A Selected List of Sources.* Stanford: Stanford University Libraries, 1981.

235. McKinley, Juanita E., ed. *Education in Tanzania: A Working Bibliography.* Stanford: Stanford University Libraries, 1981.

236. Morrison, David R. *Education and Politics in Africa: The Tanzanian Case.* London: C. Hurst and Co., 1976.

Examines education in terms of policies related to social structure, occupational integration and political integration. Material for the book was drawn from published and unpublished documents as well as over 400 interviews with politicians, civil servants and teachers. Discusses such topics as the politics of primary school expansion, the framework for policy making and the relationship between education and political socialization.

237. Mutua, Rosalind W. *Development of Education in Kenya.* Nairobi: East African Literature Bureau, 1975.

Primary emphasis is on evolving government policy during colonialism and since independence. Attention is also paid to the changes in the administrative structure.

238. Ng'ang'a, James M. *Education in Kenya since Independence: A Bibliography, 1963-83.* Nairobi: Kenyatta University College Library, 1983.

239. Ng'ang'a, James M. *Science, Technology and Education Research in Eastern Africa: A Selected Bibliography.* Nairobi: Kenyatta University College Library, 1983.

240. Prewitt, Kenneth, ed. *Education and Political Values: An East African Case Study.* Nairobi: East African Publishing House,

1971.

A collection of essays which describe how the educational systems in Kenya, Tanzania and Uganda affect political life. The two major sections include one devoted to a description of the kind of political education given primary and secondary school students in the three countries; the second, details student politics in higher education. Some chapters offer a penetrating view of how these nations want to use schooling to develop good citizens. Field research is an integral part of several chapters.

241.   Raju, Beulah M.   *Education in Kenya: Problems and Perspectives in Educational Planning and Administration.* London: Heinemann Educational Books Ltd., 1973.

The author was a UNESCO expert who spent four years at the University of Nairobi. Her area of expertise was educational planning and the primary focus of the book is in this area. Chapters are devoted to all levels of planning in formal education. The book illustrates such approaches to planning as systems analysis, diagnostic and statistical analysis and priority planning. Attention is also given to the relationship of education to society and to economic growth.

242.   Sheffield, James R.   *Education in the Republic of Kenya.* Washington: U.S. Government Printing Office, 1971.

A relatively short government publication which gives an overview of the structure and function of education. Some attention is given to education outside the formal system. Statistical information is an integral part of the study.

243.   Thias, Hans H. and Martin, Carnoy.   *Cost-Benefit Analysis in Education: A Case Study of Kenya.* Baltimore: Johns Hopkins Press, 1972.

This is a study undertaken by the World Bank and their economics department. It was preceded by a paper prepared for the Bank entitled, "A Cost-Benefit Approach to Eductional Planning in Developing Countries." This case study is a follow-up to that paper. It takes into account the income effects of education and provides a framework for an economic evaluation. The data for the study was based on interviews of almost 5,000 employees living in three urban areas. A carefully structured and very detailed case study with good use of statistical information. The authors recognize both the strengths and weaknesses in their methodological approach.

244. Umbina, W. E. *Research in Education on East Africa (Kenya, Tanzania, and Uganda) -- Periodical Articles, Theses and Research Papers, 1900-1976.* Nairobi: University of Nairobi, 1977.

245. Wolff, Laurence. *Controlling the Costs of Education in Eastern Africa: A Review of Data, Issues, and Policies.* Washington, D.C.: World Bank, 1984.

This was a World Bank Staff Working Paper that discussed such issues as investment in education, inefficiency in schools and decentralization. In some ways it was a preliminary paper to the World Bank Publication in 1986 entitled, *Financing Education in Developing Countries, An Exploration of Policy Options*.

Articles

246. Heyneman, Stephen P. "Education during a Period of Austerity: Uganda, 1971-1981." *Comparative Education Review* 27, No. 3 (1983): 403-413.

247. Hough, J. R. "Educational Development in Ethiopia." *Compare* 17, No. 2 (1987): 157-66.

Examines Ethiopia's expanding educational system under the influence of socialism. Reports on the emergence of women's education, adult literacy, community participation and the improvement of teacher education.

248. Koech, M. Kipkorir. "Kenya." *Integrated Education* 20, No. 6 (1983): 23-24.

Reviews the factors which lead to better educational opportunities for urban students. These include better equipment, earlier introduction of curricular innovations and the use of English as the language of instruction.

249. Martin, C. J. "Education and Consumption in Maragoli (Kenya): Households' Educational Strategies." *Comparative Education* 18, No. 2 (1982): 139-55.

Studies, through field research, the sustained demand for educational expansion in spite of the erosion of subsistence agriculture. Assesses how households meet the increasing cost of school fees.

250. Olembo, Jotham Ombisi. "Financing Education in Kenya."

Prospects 16, No. 3 (1986): 369-75.

Studies the financing of education during a period of economic austerity.   Reviews the efforts of the government, parents, communities and international agencies.

251.   Sifuna, Daniel N.   "Kenya, Twenty Years of Multilateral Aid."
        Prospects 13, No. 4 (1983): 481-501.

Examines the shifting of goals from an emphasis on secondary and higher education toward universal and basic education. The history of educational goals and their relationship to social factors also is reviewed.

252.   Urch, George E.   "The Role of Education in Restructuring Socialism: The Tanzanian Case." *Educational Studies (U.K.)* 15, No. 3 (1989): 213-28.

Traces the nation's commitment to socialism, identifies the causes of the present economic crisis, explores the effects of the economic crisis on the socio-political structure and analyzes how the educational system has attempted to respond to the nation's problems.

Primary Education

Books

253.   Brownstein, Lewis.   *Education and Development in Rural Kenya: A Study of Primary School Graduates*. New York: Praeger Publishers, 1972.

Represents an attempt to gather data on one of Africa's most vexing problems -- the relationship between formal education and occupation. The author focuses on 834 candidates for the 1964 Kenya Preliminary Examination, who were from four districts in Kenya. Through the use of questionnaires, the candidates are traced in an attempt to determine what happened to them. Kenya's educational policy decisions are examined in light of the study's findings.

254.   Dubbeldam, L. F. B. *The Primary School and the Community in Mwanza District Tanzania*. Groningen, The Netherlands: Wolters-Noordhoff Publishing, 1970.

A sociological study with special emphasis on the status and role of teachers and the relations between parents and the schools.   A historical survey of formal education in the Mwanza region is also included. The author was part of a six-person team under the supervision of the Center for the Study of Education in Changing Societies located in Amsterdam. The focus of the overall research project was primary education and teacher training.

255. Eshiwani, George S. *Factors Influencing Performance Among Primary and Secondary School Pupils in Western Province of Kenya: A Policy Study.* Nairobi: Bureau of Educational Research, Kenyatta University College, 1983.

256. Kinyanjui, Kabiru. *Regional and Class Inequalities in Provision of Primary Education in Kenya, 1968-73: A Historical and Socio-economic Background.* Nairobi: Institute for Development Studies, University of Nairobi, 1982.

257. Maas, Jacob van Lutsenburg and G. Criel. *Distribution of Primary School Enrollments in Eastern Africa.* Washington, D.C.: East Africa Regional Office, World Bank, 1982.

258. Omari, I.M. *Universal Primary Education in Tanzania.* Ottawa, Canada: International Development Research Centre, 1983.

Articles

259. Cleghorn, Ailie, Marilyn Merritt and Jared O. Abagi. "Language Policy and Science Instruction in Kenyan Primary Schools." *Comparative Education Review* 33, No. 1 (1989): 21-39.

Discusses the initial study of a two-year project on language instruction and language usage. Focuses on the use of English for teaching upper primary level science. The research was carried out in three schools with different locations and language usage. A carefully constructed study.

260. Heyneman, Stephen P. and Dean Janison. "Student Learning in Uganda: Textbook Availability and Other Factors." *Comparative Education Review* 24, No. 2 (1980): 206-20.

Examines pupil and school characteristics in 61 primary schools in an attempt to determine which resources account for the influence of schools on learning. Pupil characteristics examined include socioeconomic status, health and ability. School characteristics include textbook availability, teacher language ability and school physical facilities.

261. Kanyike, Lawrence K. "Success and Failure as Issues in School Provisions: the Kenyan Case." *Canadian and International Education* 7, No. 2 (1988): 31-47.

262. Mosha, Herme J. "A Reassessment of the Indicators of Primary Education Quality in Developing Countries: Emerging Evidence from Tanzania." *International Review of Education* 34, No. 1 (1988): 17-46.

263. Nkinyangi, John A. "Access to Primary Education in Kenya: The Contradictions of Public Policy." *Comparative Education Review* 26, No. 2 (1982): 199-217.

Reviews two education policies to improve opportunity for less privileged youth: the abolition of school fees and the introduction of primary boarding schools in arid and semi-arid areas. Suggests that these policies were both the cause and effect of educational failure.

Secondary Education

Books

*   Kasozi, A.B.K. *The Crisis of Secondary School Education in Uganda, 1960-1970.* Cited above as item 231.

264. Marshall, James. *A School in Uganda.* London: Victor Gollancz Ltd., 1976.

Chronicles the author's experiences as a secondary school teacher in the late 60's. Reads like a personal diary as the author attempts to reflect on his teaching and life around him. Illustrates the cross-cultural gap which exists.

Articles

265. Harty, Harold and Hassan Hassan. "Student Control Ideology and the Science Classroom Environment in Urban Secondary Schools of Sudan." *Journal of Research in Science Teaching* 20, No. 9 (1983): 851-59.

Studies the relations between science teachers' pupil control ideology and the students' perception of the psychosocial environment of their classroom. Implications for the lack of a significant relationship between the ideologies of teachers and pupil perceptions is discussed from both a Sudanese and American perception.

266. Kagia, Ruth. "Assessment: The Kenyan Case." *Studies in Educational Evaluation* 11, No. 3 (1985): 255-59.

267. Lauglo, Jon and Anders Narman. "Diversified Secondary Education in Kenya: The Status of Practical Projects, and Effects on Attitudes and Destinations After School." *International Journal of Educational Development* 7, No. 4 (1987): 227-42.

268. Saunders, Murray. "Productive Activity in the Curriculum: Changing the Literate Bias of Secondary Schools in Tanzania." *British Journal of Sociology of Education* 3, No. 1 (1982): 39-55.

Assesses efforts to modify the curriculum by unifying academic and productive work. The author suggests the new approach is not working because of the relationship between schools and the division of labor, the difficulty in determining how to unite the two areas and the problem of school organization.

269. Shiman, David A. and Kilemi Mwiria. "Struggling Against the Odds: 'Harambee' Secondary Schools in Kenya." *Phi Delta Kappan* 68, No. 5 (1987): 369-72.

Harambee schools make up 75% of all secondary schools, but only 7% of the students attending the University of Nairobi are products of these schools. The authors explore the reasons behind this statistic by examining a typical Harambee school and discuss the problems which surround it and similar schools.

270. Wellings, Paul. "Occupational and Educational Aspirations and Expectations of Kenyan Secondary School Students: Realism and Structural Inequalities." *Educational Review* 34, No. 3 (1982): 253-65.

Comments on the status of secondary schools by summarizing a recent research survey. The realism of aspirations and expectations is shown to be related to inequalities in opportunity.

Tertiary and Higher Education

Books

*   Barken, Joel D. *An African Dilemma: University Students' Development and Politics in Ghana, Tanzania and Uganda.* Cited above as item 121.

271.   Court, David. *The Idea of Social Science in East Africa: An Aspect of the Development of Higher Education.* Nairobi: Institute for Development Studies, University of Nairobi, 1981.

272.   Griffiths, V.L. *Teacher-Centered: Quality in Sudan Primary Education, 1930 to 1970.* Bristol: Longman Group Ltd, 1975.

In 1934 the author was asked to develop a training college to prepare primary teachers. This book chronicles the development of the college through the eyes of V. L. Griffiths. Attention is paid to the writing of curriculum material, the establishment of a laboratory school and the evolution of in-service training. The author also looks at the problem of content, teacher morale and relationships both internal and external. In 1969 and again in 1970, Mr. Griffiths returned to the college to determine whether what he experienced thirty or forty years ago had any relevance to educational problems faced today in developing countries. The answer was yes. An excellent account of educational development in rural Africa written by a highly respected educator.

273.   Maliyamkono, T.L., A.G.M. Ishumi and S.J. Well. *Higher Education and Development in East Africa.* London: Heinemann Educational Books Ltd., 1982.

The Eastern African Universities Research Project (EAURP) is the subject of the book. The Project's beginning in 1978, its purpose, achievements and field research are reported in detail. The Project began with a series of workshops and seminars that brought together university and government representatives, local and international experts and representatives of donor agencies. The discussions provided a theoretical framework that culminated in a research study. The study focused on individuals who had trained abroad, and paired them for a comparative analysis with individuals who had trained locally, in five occupational categories. Samples were taken from five countries, namely Kenya, Somalia, Swaziland, Tanzania and Zambia.

274.   Schoeneberger, M.M. and E.S. Odynak. *A Case Study of an International Teacher Education Program: Tanzania Project.* Edmonton: University of Alberta, 1974.

Describes and evaluates a three-year project which brought approximately 50 Tanzanian educators to the University of Alberta to study under the direction of the Faculty of Education. A special program of study was developed which emphasized primary education. Close cooperation between Tanzania and University of Alberta officials was considered an important goal to ensure the development of suitable programs based on Tanzanian needs. The evaluation describes what appeared to succeed and what appeared to fail.

275. Southall, Roger. *Federalism and Higher Education in East Africa*. Nairobi: East African Publishing House, 1974.

Examines the attempt to develop an interterritorial federal university which linked colleges in Kenya, Tanzania and Uganda between 1963 and 1970. Some excellent primary resource material is used to show the political constraints placed on the new University of East Africa. The limits of federalism in higher education are also examined. In 1970 the federal university was dissolved to make way for independent universities in each country.

Articles

276. Alladin, Ibrahim. "The University of Mauritius: Context and Evolution." *Prospects* 17, No. 2 (1987): 289-96.

277. Court, David. "The Development Ideal in Higher Education: The Experience of Kenya and Tanzania." *Higher Education* 9, No. 6 (1980): 657-80.

Comments on the potential and limits of a meaningful role for African universities in the 1980's. Observes that the challenge is to convince the government and the people that universities contribute to development through the ability to train minds necessary for a thinking society.

Specialized Education (Adult, Community, Nonformal, Technical, Vocational)

Books

278. Abreu, Elsa. *The Role of Self-Help in the Development of Education in Kenya, 1900-1973*. Nairobi: Kenya Literature Bureau, 1982.

Traces the contributions made by African and Asian voluntary organizations and assesses the role of self-help in the overall development of Kenyan education. The primary focus of the book is on the contributions of the Muslim, Hindu and Goan communities to the education of their own. A chapter also is devoted to the early independent school movement by specific African ethnic groups.

279.   Capen, B.R. *The Village Polytechnic Training Scheme in Kenya: Education for Stagnation or Development?* Norwich: School of Development Studies, University of East Anglia, 1981.

280.   Eiseman, Thomas Owen. *Benefitting from Basic Education, School Quality and Functional Literacy in Kenya.* New York: Pergamon Press, 1988.

One of a volume in a comparative and international education series that analyzes educational issues within an interdisciplinary cross-national framework. The book is based on field work conducted in the Msambweni location in coastal Kenya. The focus is on the cognitive outcomes of literacy acquisition in Koranic and secular schools in the area. The author offers a detailed description of learning tasks found in the schools which relate to the acquisition of literacy. The cognitive skills associated with these learning tasks also are examined. The book is worthy of special attention by those interested in specific ways comprehension and communication skills can be examined in rural primary schools.

281.   Gillette, Arthur L. *Beyond the Nonformal Fashion: Towards Educational Revolution in Tanzania.* Amherst: Center for International Education, University of Massachusetts, 1977.

Details the relationship between formal and nonformal education, especially in rural Tanzania. The author highlights the convergence of Nyerere's "Education for Self Reliance" with the emerging importance of nonformal education, both in the primary schools and through adult education. Chapters also discuss the organization and financing of education. Excellent use of documents and other source material.

282.   Hall, Budd L. *Adult Education and the Development of Socialism in Tanzania.* Dar es Salaam: East African Literature Bureau, 1975.

Traces the development of an adult education network from independence in 1961, through the establishment of the Institute of Adult Education in the Ministry of Education. The author investigates the hypothesis that adult education has undergone changes in function and emphasis as a result of the government's commitment to socialism. Chapters explore this hypothesis and go beyond in describing some of the approaches used in specific campaigns.

283.   Johnsson, A. I., K. Nystrom and R. Sunden. *Adult Education*

in Tanzania. Stockholm: Swedish International Development Authority, 1983.

One in a series of education documents published by SIDA. It reviews the educational programs sponsored by the Swedish government.

284. Kaayk, Jan. *Education, Estrangement and Adjustment.* The Hague: Mouton and Co., 1976.

A study among pupils and school teachers in Bukumbi, a rural community in Tanzania. The goal of the study was to collect facts at the grass roots level which could provide practical recommendations for educational reform. The author analyzes education in relation to rural development, employment and migration while taking into consideration the socio-economic and psychological problems of the youth involved. The book is one of a series sponsored by the Center for the Study of Education in Changing Societies, The Hague. The series attempts to analyze primary education in relation to rural development.

285. King, Kenneth. *The African Artisan: Education and the Informal Sector in Kenya.* London: Heinemann Educational Books Ltd., 1977.

Focuses on the informal education of skilled artisans found in the manufacturing side of the economy. Shows how schools and skills drifted apart. Traces informal skill development against a background of attempts by the government to produce skilled manpower. Illustrations came from specific case studies. Should be of special interest to nonformal educators who want to look beyond rural development.

286. Niehoff, Richard O. and B. C. Wilder. *Programs of Studies in Non-Formal Education: Non-Formal Education in Ethiopia.* East Lansing: Institute for International Studies in Education, Michigan State University, 1974.

One of a series of team reports designed to build a systematic knowledge base on nonformal education. The two-person team in Ethiopia was part of the University's Program of Studies in Non-Formal Education. The Program produced nearly 100 working papers. Reports represented in this volume range from observations and case studies of nonformal projects, to the role of nonformal education within the country's formal structure, to a review of proposals for the implementation of projects in rural areas.

*   Okeem, E.D.   *Adult Education in Ghana and Tanzania,*
         1945-75. Cited above as item 145.

287.   Sifuna, Daniel. *The Dilemma of Technical Education in Kenya:*
         A Historical Study. Nairobi: Kenyatta University College,
         1983.

288.   UNICEF.   *Survey of Basic Education in Eastern Africa.*
         Nairobi: UNICEF, Eastern Africa Regional Office, 1980.

Articles

289.   Bennell, Paul.   "Occupational Transfer: A Case Study of
         Craft-Training Policies in Kenya, 1945-1980." *Comparative*
         Education Review 28, No. 1 (1984): 28-51.

Discusses the evolution of policies and practices with particular
reference to engineering traders.   Provides a case study of
occupational and training transfer from Britain.   Explores the
relations between training and the labor market.

290.   Cameron, John.   "Education, Individuality and
         Community-Education for Self-Reliance in Tanzania." *British*
         Journal of Educational Studies 28, No. 2 (1980): 100-11.

Reviews the social, cultural, religious and political influences in order
to consider self-reliance from a better perspective. Also discusses the
precept and practice of education for self-reliance.

291.   Coldwvin, G.O. "Broadcasting Development and Research in
         Kenya." *Journal of Educational Television and Other Media* 6,
         No. 2 (1980): 61-66.

Examines the development and use of educational broadcasting since
independence.   The major projects are reviewed and analyzed,
especially those relating to the use of radio.

292.   Donnan, Graeme E. "The Slopes of Kilimanjaro: Teaching
         Experientially in Tanzania." *Journal of Experiential Education*
         8, No. 2 (1985): 23-27.

Describes the experiential learning curriculum at the International
School in Moshi. Discusses the objectives, organization and benefits
of this outdoor program which takes advantage of the environmental
features of the area.

293. Eisemon, Thomas Owen, Elkana Ong'esa and Lynn Hart. "Schooling for Self-Employment in Kenya: The Acquisiton of Crafts Skills in and Outside Schools." *International Journal of Educational Development* 8, No. 4 (1988): 271-78.

294. Gichuru, F.X. "Basic Education for Street Children in Nairobi." *Prospects* 17, No. 1 (1987): 139-42.

295. Godia, George. "Educational Expansion and Economic Development in Kenya." *Journal of Studies in Technical Careers* 8, No. 1 (1986): 61-72.

Challenges the high priority given to formal education in light of high unemployment. Suggests broadening the curriculum to include vocational training.

296. Holmberg, Borge. "Applications of Distance Education in Kenya." *Distance Education* 6, No. 2 (1985): 242-47.

Suggests several conditions that work against the development of distance education. Describes three programs that have been planned and implemented in the 1980's and discusses what is being achieved in each of the programs. The programs described are an inservice course for primary school teachers, a basic course for adult literacy and a paramedical training course.

297. Maliyamkono, T.L. "The School as a Force for Community Change in Tanzania." *International Review of Education* 26, No. 3 (1980): 335-47.

Studies two reform programs, 'Education for Self-Reliance' and 'Decentralization'. Comments on their relevance to rural life, and the promotion of community participation. The article notes the importance of adult education.

298. Mosha, H.J. "United Republic of Tanzania: Folk Development Colleges." *Prospects* 13, No. 1 (1983): 95-103.

Describes the program development and implementation of colleges based on the Swedish folk high schools. The schools were started to help students develop their personality and culture and gain a better understanding of national and international affairs.

299. Mushi, P.A.K. "Cultural Beliefs and Utilization of Functional Literacy Skills in Tanzania." *Perspectives in Education* 3, No. 2 (1987): 11-16.

300.   Narman, Anders.   "Technical Secondary Schools and the Labour Market: Some Results of a Tracer Study in Kenya." *Comparative Education* 24, No. 1 (1988):   19-35.

301.   Sifuna, Daniel.   "Unemployment and Non-Formal Training in the Informal Sector in Kenya." *Education with Production* 5, No. 1 (1986): 40-57.

Reviews educational projects that are tailored toward training and the world of work. The emphasis is on non-institutional activities. Also contains a general overview of the unemployment problem in Kenya.

302.   waMirie, Nugugi.   "Literacy for and by the People: Kenya's Kamirithu Project." *Convergence* 13, No. 4 (1980):   51-55.

Examines a specific literacy program and relates the importance of integrating the program into the process of community development.

Curriculum and Methods

Books

303.   Kimball, Richard L. *An Inquiry into the Relationship Between a New Science Curriculum and Creative Growth, Uganda.* Stanford: Stanford International Development Education Center, 1971.

Explores the problem of maladjustment resulting from rapid change and attempts to understand the forces causing change. The author studied male children and adults to determine whether specific forms of science education could help identify the change and mobilize resources and strategies to successfully adapt to it. Three forms of science education included in the study were observation, problem-solving and experimentation.

304.   Mbuyi, Dennis M. *Beyond Policy and Language Choice: An Analysis of Texts in Four Instructional Contexts in East Africa.* Buffalo: Comparative Education Center, State University of New York at Buffalo, 1987.

Articles

305.   Berger, Ian R. and Simon Ngaliwa.   "*Mradi Wa Afya Mashuleni*": The Tanzania School Health Program." *Journal of School Health* 53, No. 2 (1983): 95-98.

Comments on the program and its goals which are to improve the health of primary school students, extend health benefits to school villages and test strategies to expand the program nationally.

306. Briggs, John and Alex Gray. "Geography in a Developing Country: The Case of the University of Dar es Salaam, Tanzania." *Journal of Geography in Higher Education* 6, No. 1 (1982): 39-46.

Describes the college level geography instruction and reviews the type of careers pursued by graduates, secondary school teachers and resource assessors.

307. Eisemon, Thomas Owen, Vimla Patel and J. Abagi. "Read These Instructions Carefully: Examination Reform and Improving Health Education in Kenya." *International Journal of Educational Development* 8, No. 1 (1988): 55-66.

308. Feldman, Robert H.L. "Communicating Nutrition to High School Students in Kenya." *Journal of School Health* 53, No. 2 (1983): 140-43.

Discusses a study which examines the effectiveness of different combinations of teacher expertise and teacher-audience.

309. Rasimali, Jaffer. "Language Choice in East Africa." *Social Education* 49, No. 2 (1985): 111-112.

Comments on the different approaches to language usage in the schools. Notes the overwhelming use of Swahili in Tanzania while the other East African countries have turned to the use of the colonial languages.

310. Lillis, Kevin M. "Processes of Secondary Curriculum Innovation in Kenya." *Comparative Education Review* 29, No. 1 (1985): 80-96.

Follows the course of two innovations in the schools and discusses the reasons for the problems which surrounded them. The two innovations were the School Mathematics of East Africa Program and the Africanization of the literature curriculum.

311. Lillis, Kevin M. "Africanizing the School Literature Curriculum in Kenya: A Case Study in Curriculum Dependency." *Journal of Curriculum Studies* 18, No. 1 (1986): 63-84.

Focuses on attempts made during the 1970's to achieve greater cultural autonomy through curriculum revision.   Gives specific reasons for the problems associated with the attempts.

312.   Lillis, Kevin M. and John Lowe.   "The Rise and Fall of the Schools Science Project in East Africa." *Compare* 17, No. 2 (1987): 167-79.

Studies the problems associated with the implementation of a new science project in the 1970's.   Chronicles its downfall and gives reasons why.   Raises additional questions concerning the teaching of science in the developing world.

313.   Maple, Terry L.   "Comparative Psychology as an East African Field Course." *Teaching of Psychology* 8, No. 4 (1981): 237-41.

Describes a comparative psychology course in which college students learn through the observation of animals in their natural habitats. The focus is on Kenya.

314.   McCormick, R.   "Political Education as Moral Education in Tanzania." *Journal of Moral Education* 9, No. 3 (1980): 66-77.

Considers the issues of citizenship, socialism and development within political education.   Explores the effects of this education and the problems associated with indoctrination.

315.   Merryfield, M.M.   "Curricular Reform in Kenyan Primary Schools: A Comparison of Classroom Instruction in Social Studies with Geography, History and Civics." *Kenya Journal of Education* 3, No. 1 (1986): 64-84.

Reviews a Primary Education Project designed to integrate the separate subjects into social studies.   Concludes that the Project was successful, but questions whether the idea could be implemented nationally.

316.   Saigh, Philip A.   "School Psychology in the Sudan." *Journal of School Psychology* 25, No. 3 (1987): 281-85.

Contains information on the system of education, the practice of school psychology and its administration.   Examines its contributions and the problems associated with it.

Teachers

Book

317. Karugu, A.M. *Primary School Teachers in Kenya: A Study of Teachers' Views on Promotion.* Nairobi: Bureau of Educational Research, Kenyatta University College, 1982.

Article

318. Lindsay, Beverly. "Redefining the Educational and Cultural Milieu of Tanzanian Teachers: A Case Study in Development or Dependency?" *Comparative Education* 25, No. 1 (1989): 87-96.

Examines the role of secondary school teachers and their training in a specific American sponsored program to adjudge the consequences on development and dependency. A case study of a Teacher-Text-Technology project in Tanzania also is analyzed to determine its relationship to the educational and cultural milieu of teachers and teacher trainers. The case is a three-year initiative undertaken by the University of Massachusetts Center for International Education to strengthen the teaching of science, math, and English in the secondary schools.

Religion and Private Education

Article

319. Samoff, Joel. "School Expansion in Tanzania: Private Initiative and Public Policy." *Comparative Education Review* 31, No. 3 (1987): 333-60.

Details the expansion of private education, both primary and secondary. Analyzes reasons behind the expansion. Utilizes case studies and statistical information. Field research adds to the careful documentation of the article.

Education for Women

Books

320. Adams, Milton N. and Susan E. Kruppenbach. *Some Issues of Access and Equality in the Education of African Females: Progress and Prospects.* East Lansing: Michigan State University, 1986.

321. Eshiwani, George S. *A Study of Woman's Access to Higher*

Education in Kenya with a Special Reference to Mathematics and Science Education. Nairobi: Bureau of Educational Research, Kenyatta University College, 1983.

322. Luguga, Lucy. *Training and Employment Opportunities for Out-of-School Girls in Dar es Salaam.* Addis Ababa: United Nations Economic Commission for Africa, 1984.

Article

323. Pollitt, A.B. and Others. "Factors Affecting Girls' Learning of Mathematics in Sudan." *Educational Studies in Mathematics* 18, No. 4 (1987): 439-44.

Describes the effects of a mathematics program and a self-learning project on the learning of mathematics by girls. Draws some comparisons between boys and girls.

SOUTHERN AFRICA

Independence came late to most parts of Southern Africa and the confrontation more severe between the colonizer and the colonized. The Portuguese colonies of Angola and Mozambique gained independence in 1975, and then only after a long armed struggle and a political coup in Portugal. Zimbabwe did not become independent until 1980 and, once again, only after a long and bloody war of liberation. The latest nation to gain its independence in the area is Namibia, which finally saw its own flag raised in 1990. The long and arduous struggle is still on the minds of the leaders and their people.

The slow emergence of majority rule can be explained in part by European domination of the area both politically and economically. The Portuguese were early European explorers of the continent and early colonizers. Both of their colonies had a well entrenched white minority who governed with a heavy hand. White dominated Rhodesia was similar. British immigration, to Rhodesia, now called Zimbabwe, began after World War I and continued well into the 1950's by which time much of the most arable land became the property of the colonizer. Until the mid-1970's the triple alliance of Portugal, Rhodesia, and South Africa dominated the area politically, militarily and economically. Western collusion with this minority and privileged group of Europeans helped to create suspicion and alienation between the new leaders and Western countries.

With independence the emergence of new governments has helped to form new alliances, some for political reasons and others for economic opportunities. The primary political reason for the alliance of some "front line" states is the continuing struggle to liberate the rest of the continent from minority rule, namely South Africa. The need to join forces against the common enemy of a racist South Africa has brought governments together that do not share a common ideology. Both Angola and Mozambique have moved toward a Marxist-Leninist regime while Botswana, Zambia and Zimbabwe appear to be pursuing state capitalism.

Economically the southern part of the continent is a region where such natural resources as mineral wealth, water and arable land are not distributed equally. Neither are the developed resources of agriculture, industry, transportation and educated person power. As a consequence it is difficult for the new nations to pursue independent economic paths. For some nations there is still an economic interdependence with South Africa as well as dependency on the world market for the price of minerals. Several countries are endeavoring to develop mutually beneficial economic ties. However, the long struggle for independence has brought dislocation and neglect to economic development. The road back is just beginning.

Education in the region is dramatically affected by independence. Several of the new states quickly moved away from the inherited colonial pattern. The most dramatic change has taken place in the two former Portuguese colonies. Both have ousted the European teachers and their system. In their place is the beginning of a structure that emphasizes rural based education and a focus on functional literacy. In Zimbabwe educational opportunity at the secondary level had been minimal and the new leaders have embarked on a massive expansion. Zambia has introduced a new theme of 'Humanism" in an attempt to move away from an elite urban based system and take opportunity into rural areas. Other states are still searching for a direction that will provide political stability and economic development. It is in this backdrop that education in the region can best be understood.

ANGOLA

Overview

When the liberation movement gained independence in 1975 it established a socialist form of government based on the ideology of Marxism-Leninism. This meant state ownership of most means of production and central planning. However, much of the private sector is permitted to continue joint enterprises in the exploration of oil and other natural resources. Angola's richness in mineral and oil deposits gives it an economic potential not shared by many countries on the continent. The strong economic base bodes well for the future development of education. However, the new nation must begin its educational development from the ground level.

During the colonial period African Angolans had very little access to education. With a population of over seven million people most government funds went toward the education of the 400,000 European population and the few "assimilados" living in urban areas. They attended schools based on those in Portugal with the language of instruction Portuguese. Some mission education was available for the Africans in rural areas, but colonial financial support was almost non-existent. When independence came there was a massive exodus of the European population, including Portuguese teachers, and the educational system virtually ceased to exist.

During the struggle for independence the liberation movement had established the semblance of an educational structure in the rural areas they controlled. Much of it was based on practical application to rural problems and on political education. The ideas used in these early attempts were soon transferred to the new government.

Structure

One of the first steps the national government took was to reform the structure and control of education. The new system is based on the Marxist-Leninist philosophy with respect for African traditions and values. All schools are nationalized and productive work is being introduced into all levels of education.

The Ministry of Education administers a highly centralized system and has direct control over the primary, middle and secondary levels. The responsibility for vocational education is shared among several ministries and adult education is managed by a National Literacy Center. The educational ladder begins with a basic 4 year primary cycle followed by the two upper components of 2 years each for a total of 8 years. Students then can enter one of five types of middle or secondary education. There is a 2-year pre-university program and four 4-year programs that specialize in supplying the nation's technical needs to support national development. Teacher training also is one of the programs. Vocational training of 3 years duration begins after 6 years of primary education. At the top of the educational ladder is the newly renamed University of Agostino Nieto. Many of the former Portuguese instructors are being replaced by Soviet and Eastern European professors as well as a few from Brazil.

Function

The Ministry's Center for Pedagogical Research is responsible for developing the curriculum as well as the production of textbooks. The new curriculum is to focus on the education of a political, technical and scientific cadre as well as a program to eradicate illiteracy estimated to be 85% of the adult population. This means that in addition to the basic subjects, work related courses and political education can be found at all levels. Attempts are being made to indigenize the language of instruction in the rural primary schools, but Portuguese is still used at the middle and higher levels.

Angola suffers from an acute shortage of trained teachers which slows progress. Some teachers are being imported from Cuba and Brazil as well as Eastern Europe, but not in sufficient numbers.

Mandatory conscription into the military for all 18 year olds also handicaps the training of teachers.

The country suffered from a long period of civil war that destroyed much of the nation's infra-structure and killed many of its potential leaders. Once normalcy returns, the future for education could be bright given political stability and the nation's strong economic base.

BOTSWANA

Overview

This was one of three countries in southern Africa that was declared a British Protectorate when the Republic of South Africa gained its independence from Great Britain. The Kalahari Desert makes up 80% of the land surface in this large country. One consequence is that approximately 80% of the 1.2 million people live near the Limpopo River. Since independence in 1966, a diamond boom has brought unprecedented economic prosperity. This prosperity, a stable and democratic oriented government and the homogeneity of the people, are all positive factors that help to promote educational development. On the other hand, the prosperity is bringing a huge population growth, a rush into quickly growing urban areas and a growing division between those who have benefitted from the prosperity and educational opportunity and those who have not. To deal with these problems and to oversee the development of education the government in 1976 formed a policy making National Commission on Education. Their first report was based on the nation's slogan of "Kagisano" or social harmony.

Structure

The educational system is given the responsibility to promote the nation's four national principles -- democracy, development, self-reliance and unity. To help meet this responsibility over one-fourth of the national budget is committed to its development. The system is administered jointly by the Ministry of Education, who manages all levels of education, except the university, and the Ministry of Local Government and Lands, who provides finances for the development and maintenance of primary school buildings. The administration of the primary schools is through the local district education officers who report to the Ministry. Secondary schools are supervised directly by the central Ministry. The government made universal primary education and literacy its major educational goals. To help in meeting these goals an Accelerated Rural Development Programme has been initiated that is designed to improve the facilities and teaching. The educational ladder is presently in transition from a 7 - 3 - 2 structure to a 6 - 3 - 3 plan. However much of the transition has not yet taken place. Since 1986, junior secondary schools either have been 2 or 3 years in duration depending upon their subject matter orientation. The University of Botswana tops the educational ladder. Admission to the four faculties is through the Cambridge Overseas School Certificate examination. Many university students pursue studies at other African universities or study overseas.

The country has a strong nonformal education component directed by the Department of Nonformal Education within the Ministry. The Department not only helps to develop literacy programs, but offers correspondence courses that lead to secondary school certificates. The best known nonformal education programs are the Botswana Brigades formed in the mid-1960's by Patrick van Rensburg. They offer an alternative to formal secondary education through vocational education closely associated with local production needs. By the 1980's there were 18 brigade centers training youth in rural areas.

Function

The primary schools teach a nationally prescribed curriculum that does allow some adaptation to local conditions. The program is designed to make the curriculum more practical, especially in reference to agriculture. Children begin their education in Setswana, the mother tongue for over 80% of the population, and then switch to English usually in the third or fourth year. The rapid expansion of primary schools has left a severe shortage of trained teachers. The secondary school curriculum is determined by academic oriented external examinations, although every school is required to offer one practical subject. The rapid expansion of secondary schools has produced a severe shortage of teachers at this level as well. Many of the teachers are expatriates who come to Botswana on 2-3 year contracts.

As yet the secondary schools have not diversified their curriculum to the extent that they can meet the demand for mid-level technicians needed in the exploration of the nation's mineral wealth. The nation's high level manpower needs also are not being met through higher education. This is one challenge the system must assume. Another challenge is to provide the necessary teachers, textbooks and classroom materials needed to meet the rapid expansion. However, the biggest challenge is to maintain the national philosophy of "Kagisano" social harmony, in the face of rapid social and economic change.

LESOTHO

Overview

The kingdom of Lesotho is a former British Protectorate that occupies a mountainous area which is completely surrounded by the Republic of South Africa. It is one of the smallest and less developed countries on the continent. Besides a few mineral deposits and hydroelectric power, it has few resources to help aid its development. Much of the country's infrastructure depends upon South Africa and approximately 40% of its Gross National Product is derived from the men who labor in the mines of South Africa. The resident population is primarily rural and is engaged in subsistence agriculture in the lowlands and cattle raising in some of the mountains.

The country is blessed with an homogenous population. Over 85% of the people are Basotho who speak the language of Sesotho. The common language has made it possible to produce reading material and encourage schooling. As a consequence the country has one of the highest literacy rates on the continent. Through the efforts of the government and religious groups the country also enjoys a fairly well developed system of education that includes a primary school within walking distance of almost all of the population.

Structure

The administration of the schools is a joint venture between the government and the Christian churches. Over 90% of all primary schools and over 80% of the secondary schools are owned and operated by churches. The government assists these schools by supervising them and paying the teachers' salaries including in-service training. A portion of the costs of maintaining the schools also is assumed by the government.

The Ministry of Education, Youth, Sports, and Culture educates and appoints teachers, administers the external examinations and authorizes the curriculum. It is assisted by a central inspectorate division and ten district education officers who maintain contact with the school managers. The educational ladder begins with 7 years of primary education that culminates in an external examination. While virtually all children have access to a primary school, not all of them have the full 7 years. General secondary education consists of a 3-year junior cycle followed by a 2-year senior cycle for those who successfully complete the Junior Certificate Examination. In the

1970's well over half the students attending primary and secondary schools were young women, but the trend in the 1980's saw more young men attending school for a longer period of time. The system is topped by the National University of Lesotho which opened in 1975. The present enrollment at the University is relatively small.

Function

A National Curriculum Development Center helps to develop syllabi and materials for a required core curriculum at both the primary and secondary level. In most primary schools children begin instruction in Sesotho and switch to English around the 4th year. Beyond the 4th year all instruction is in English. The domination of the church in the educational system ensures religious instruction at all levels. The system is criticized as being too academic and the government is attempting to vocationalize it. Six experimental secondary schools diversified their curriculum in the 1980's and offer more practical subjects. The vocationalization program also helps one of the technical institutes to upgrade itself to a polytechnic. The University now offers diploma courses in agriculture and home economics.

One of the strengths of the education system is the complementary nonformal sector that reaches out to the rural areas. The Lesotho Distance Teaching Center, which opened in the mid-70's, promotes outreach and the government provides funds for small organizations involved in nonformal education. Their efforts are supplemented by the Institute of Extra-Mural Studies located at the University. The Institute reaches out into rural areas with both basic education and formal part-time course work. In addition, the Ministry of Agriculture operates six farmer training centers, each of which has a demonstration farm.

The overall system faces several challenges which must be met with limited funds. The quality of the teachers is a concern as is the need to make education more practical. Fortunately the government receives funds from international organizations to help meet these challenges.

MALAWI

Overview

The country is one of several land-locked countries on the continent that is dependent upon other nations for its trade with the outside world. Its lack of natural resources and dependency on its neighbors continue to make Malawi one of the countries with the lowest Gross National Product in the world. The lack of economic opportunity for its population of seven million has caused large numbers of young men to seek employment outside its borders. The young men recognize that employment opportunities are linked to the amount of education they bring with them and as a consequence seek and value educational opportunity.

The nation enjoys good agricultural land, where 95% of the people live. Since independence in 1964 there has been a steady rise in agricultural productivity. The government recognizes the importance of promoting development in this area and educational policy emphasizes agricultural and rural development at all levels.

Structure

The Ministry of Education and Culture has complete authority over education at all levels except the national university. It operates with the help of regional and district officers who share responsibility for their areas. Certain aspects of primary education have been decentralized and responsibility given to the town or city council which has been declared a local educational authority. Local communities contribute to education by constructing primary schools often through self-help projects. Their efforts are coordinated with missionary groups, which pioneered primary education and still have proprietorship over many schools. Throughout the country Christian missionary influence is strong.

Primary education consists of 8 years divided into 5 years of junior primary and 3 years of senior primary. Some experimentation is taking place within the primary cycle and the movement appears to be toward shortening the number of years. Only 15% of primary school leavers go on to secondary schools that offer 4 years of study followed by a specialized British style sixth form for 2 additional years. The prestigious secondary schools are still boarding schools and over 90% of the students who attend them complete the course of study. Because of increased demand for secondary education day schools are now being built, but the drop out rate is high, especially among young women. The educational ladder is topped by the University of Malawi, an umbrella institution which is responsible for colleges located in different parts of the country. The colleges include those with primary responsibility for agriculture, education and nursing.

Function

Since independence the country has emphasized the development of a system that can contribute to the increased production of the land. The primary school curriculum caters directly to the needs of a rural society. Agriculture, home economics and craft technology are introduced in the upper levels and science is geared toward the needs of a rural society. The initial language of instruction is Chichewa, the national language. The switch to English begins in the upper primary level, if not sooner, and continues through secondary and higher education.

The secondary curriculum also is diversified. Agriculture is a compulsory subject and mechanical subjects such as wood and metal work for boys and home economics for girls are being introduced. The elite secondary schools still maintain a solid academic oriented curriculum that prepares students for higher education. Enrollment in higher education is limited since most of the resources go into primary and secondary education. Nonformal education operates through an extensive extension service and plays an important role in promoting rural development schemes. Eight of the ministries are involved in rural development, including agriculture, labor, health, and community development and social welfare. In addition to the work of the ministries the government organizes a national youth movement called the Malawi Young Pioneers. They are trained to improve agricultural techniques and assist in community development. They also receive some military training. Graduates are assigned to teaching and development work.

Malawi is often cited as an example of a nation that has structured its educational system to support development in rural areas. Many countries on the continent pay lip service to this, but Malawi has shown the advantage of this through increased agricultural production.

MOZAMBIQUE

Overview

Similar to Angola, the other former major Portuguese colony on the continent, Mozambique gained its independence in 1975 after a long armed struggle. Also similar to Angola the new leaders opted for a socialist form of government and used education to promote the new system. Prior to independence very little education was available for the indigenous people. The little that was available was operated by Catholic missionaries. Their primary schools emphasized the Portuguese language and culture as well as religion and helped to prepare students for skilled labor positions. Very little secondary education was available.   At the time of independence it was estimated that the illiteracy rate was at least 95%.

During the struggle for independence the emerging leaders began to develop an educational infrastructure in the rural areas under their control.   These rural schools emphasized political and basic education as well as cultural identity.   The Mozambican refugees who lived in Tanzania also established schools to help prepare educated leaders when independence came.

Structure

With independence all schools were nationalized and a highly centralized system put in place administered by the Ministry of Education and Culture.   The new constitution gave priority to adult literacy and primary education where the curriculum emphasizes agricultural and vocational training as well as political education.   All schools are free and open to all, and the new leaders emphasize the "obligation" to attend school.   During the 1980's education was second only to defense in the amount of government money it received.

Since 1983 the national system includes a 7-year primary cycle divided into the first 5 years and followed by 2 more.   Secondary education consists of an additional 7 years.   Complementary vocational and teacher training is being developed along side academic oriented schools.   At the top of the ladder is the Eduardo Mondlane University named after the national hero.

The numbers attending formal schools increased dramatically during the 1980's.   A special emphasis is being placed on enrolling young women in schools, an opportunity that was denied them under colonialism.   Literacy education for adults also is receiving attention with cadres of young people trained to promote literacy through rural community committees.

Function

The new curriculum is designed to promote the socialization of the countryside.   Practical courses, including manual labor, receive emphasis as does political education.   The national economy is supported by agriculture and particular attention is paid to it.   Many schools are developing farms alongside them.   The collectivization of farms is being emphasized.

Portuguese remains the language of instruction at all levels. While some criticism is levied at the government for maintaining the colonial language, there is not a single African language understood by the majority of the people. The country is composed of more than ten major ethnic groups each with a language that is unrelated. The government is producing its own textbooks in order that classroom material emphasize an African and socialist perspective.

Economic problems, produced in part by food shortages, are slowing the pace of educational development. However the government has a clear set of goals that highlight the relationship of education to rural economic development.

NAMIBIA

Overview

Namibia is the newest independent country on the continent. Independence came to this sparsely inhabited nation in 1990 after a long and bitter armed conflict. Originally a German colony, after World War I it became a Trust Territory of South Africa. As a consequence it fell under white minority rule and the apartheid system of separation. During the independence struggle a government in exile was formed and in 1976 a United Nations Institute for Namibia was established in Zambia. The Institute assumed responsibility for training mid-level public administrators that could manage the nation when independence came. The Director of that Institute is the present Prime Minister. Through the Institute the leadership in exile had time to discuss the kind of educational system they planned to put in place. Education was viewed as a liberating force for both men and women as well as a training ground for the development of needed human resources.

Current thinking places a heavy emphasis on basic education for all with an emphasis on literacy and numeracy. The overall literacy rate is estimated to be around 30%. The foundation is being laid for a free and universal education for all citizens from primary through secondary education. The need to urgently train technical and professional personnel, including teachers, is recognized and provisions are being made for work-oriented education for adults.

The new government has the opportunity to learn from the experiences of other African countries in building a new educational structure and process. The direction it takes will be observed by both theoreticians and practitioners.

SWAZILAND

Overview

This former British High Commission Territory is one of the smallest and least populated countries on the continent. It is surrounded on three sides by South Africa and on the fourth by Mozambique. Since its independence in 1968 the country has enjoyed political stability and a fairly even distribution of its modest wealth. The population of less than one million people is very homogeneous with over 95% sharing a common language and tradition. Over 75% of the people earn their living through agriculture although there is a growing commercial section based primarily on iron mining and forestry. Marketing is helped by an excellent infrastructure of roads as well as a railroad, and a government policy of non-alignment that permits trade with its neighbors and those beyond.

Structure

All schools, colleges and the university are under the jurisdiction of the Ministry of Education that operates through four district education officers. The education officers are assisted by chief inspectors who visit the schools to evaluate and monitor the educational quality. The good system of paved roads and a compact country assist the government in directly reaching out to the schools when new initiatives are undertaken. The government owns the majority of the secondary schools, but only 20% of the primary schools. Most of the others are operated by Christian religious groups and are government-aided. The educational ladder consists of 7 years of primary education followed by 5 years of secondary. External examinations, patterned after the British model, are given to determine access to more formal education. They are administered after grade 7, and at the end of 3 years of junior secondary school and again at the end of the 5th year. Large numbers drop out after each examination although the majority leave school before completing primary education. Half of the rural primary schools do not offer the full 7-year program. The University is modest in size and grew out of the breakup of the University of Botswana, Lesotho, and Swaziland in 1976. Presently there are two separate campuses in the country. Students tend to be sent out of the country for specialized training.

In 1975 the National Education Commission issued a report that established goals for the system. Universal free primary education is the main goal. Also included were goals to educate more primary school teachers and to develop a primary curriculum development program that would produce specific guidelines and syllabi. Special emphasis also is placed on the development of nonformal education programs for literacy and community and vocational education in rural areas.

Function

The government is attempting to use the schools in its modernization and development efforts. This means the introduction of practical and vocational courses along with conventional academic subjects. The introduction of practical subjects at the secondary level is hindered by the examination system. The schools' language policy is simplified by the homogeneous population. During the first four years students study in their mother tongue of Siswati and then switch to English for all further education. Recently schools in urban areas are using English as the medium of instruction from the first day. This is occurring for economic reasons since the language of government and business is English. A shortage of books in Siswati also makes this necessary.

Special efforts to reach out into the rural areas include the establishment of nine rural education centers that offer subjects related to the improvement of life in rural communities. The centers also offer specially designed adult literacy programs, many of which operate out of the University's Department of Extramural Studies, and educational radio broadcasting from the national system.

Swaziland is making steady educational progress since independence. It is being handicapped by a fast growing birth rate and a high drop out rate as well as a lack of qualified teachers. However, a stable government and a clear educational direction have helped the system to develop.

ZAMBIA

Overview

Zambia is often cited as a nation that relied too much and too long on a one product economy. That product is copper which produces over 80% of the nation's foreign exchange earnings. When its value dropped on the world market in the late 1970's the nation's economy suffered and it continues to suffer. The problem is compounded by movement into the urban areas where 40% of the population now resides. This drift has deterred agricultural development, deprived rural areas of leadership, and strained the urban infrastructure and social services. It also is dividing the country into an urban elite, where there is more educational opportunity, and the rural dwellers, where educational development is lagging. One result is that education is serving as a divisive rather than an integrating force. Another result is a growing number of unemployed secondary school leavers who have little to do.

Another divisive force is language. There are over 70 different languages and dialects with eleven major language groups. Seven of the languages are taught in the schools. However, English is the official language of the government and urban business. Its use is a unifying factor.

Another unifying factor is a stable political system as well as the government's commitment to provide more and equal educational opportunity. When Zambia gained its independence from Great Britain few citizens had completed secondary or higher education. What money was available for education during the colonial period tended to go toward the education of the European colonists. The new government developed its own brand of "Humanism" which links work and study and attempts to eliminate class barriers through educational expansion. By the mid 1970's free universal primary education was available to over 70% of school aged children and enrollment in secondary schools was growing faster than any other African nation. Unfortunately a precipitous drop in the price of copper slowed the expansion and began the drift into urban areas.

Structure

In 1982, the Ministry of Education and Culture was divided into the Ministry of General Education and Culture, responsible for primary, secondary, and adult education; and the Ministry of Higher Education, responsible for tertiary education and the university. The ministries manage nine educational regions that are further divided into districts. There are both national as well as regional inspectors of schools that monitor the day to day operation. Under the current decentralization plan responsibility for primary education lies with the regions for both current and capital expenditures. The system is primarily financed by the government. However, at the secondary level the government encourages the development of self-help schools. Community reaction has been positive and contributions of cash, materials and labor have greatly expanded access to secondary education. With Zambia's continuing economic difficulty it is likely that private support for education will continue to grow.

The structure of primary and secondary education also was changed in 1982. Primary education was to begin at age 7 and last 9 rather than 7 years. The last two years are generally referred to as junior secondary. Some rural primary schools only go through the first 4 years. Secondary education continues for 3 years through grade 12. The primary cycle concludes with a leaving examination. In principle there are no failures as all students receive a certificate that shows the courses they completed and their grades. Approximately 15-20% of primary school graduates enter secondary schools. There also are school leaving examinations administered after junior and senior secondary school. The University of Zambia caps the formal system. It has three campuses and consists of eight schools and a center for continuing education.

Function

All primary schools follow the Zambia Primary Course curriculum developed by the Curriculum Development Center located in the capital. Materials and textbooks to correspond with the curriculum are published and distributed by the Kenneth Kaunda Foundation, a semi-government organization. Although some primary schools, primarily in rural areas, begin schooling in one of the seven official languages, the movement is toward the use of English as a medium of instruction from the first day. Annual school examinations are given, but students do not repeat a grade if they fail.

At the secondary level attempts are being made to link practical and work related courses with academic subjects, but the school leaving examinations are a hindrance. At the senior secondary level the syllabus is primarily set by the Zambia Examinations Council. Efforts are being made to establish a technical training system and every good sized town has a trade school. In addition to the university there are several trade training institutes and higher institutes that offer 2-4 year diploma courses in such areas as public administration, medical assistants, nursing, mining and agriculture.

The government has established a clear educational philosophy and goals to help meet it. A structure also is in place. Needed is an economic resurgence to help expand the structure to meet the educational demands of a fast growing population. Whether the economic development will occur depends upon the price of copper, the extraction of other mineral deposits and attention to agricultural development.

ZIMBABWE

Overview

Zimbabwe gained its independence in 1980 after a long and destructive war between African liberation movements and the white settler colonial regime. It inherited an educational system that had been organized along racial lines with separate schools for separate races, and where provisions for the education of Africans was limited by design and finances.   When independence came the new government announced its intention to reconstruct the nation according to the tenets of "scientific socialism." Education was to be an effective vehicle to aid in this transformation. The goals were to develop a socialist consciousness among students that would help to eliminate the distinction between manual and mental work while fostering cooperative learning and opportunities for productive employment.   In addition the schools were charged with the responsibility to adapt the subject matter to Zimbabwean culture and to develop a common national identity.

To accomplish these goals the government directed its efforts toward educational expansion with particular emphasis on secondary education. Priority was initially given to the reopening of the rural schools closed during the war. This constituted nearly one-third of all the schools. Attention was then turned to the development of new schools through the efforts of parents and communities that were expected to contribute fees and labor for school construction. Private support was given freely from the belief that education would open opportunities for their children to obtain wage earning jobs in the modern sector.

During the first decade of independence enrollment increased dramatically at both the primary and secondary level. By 1990 fees were abolished at the primary level and the country had achieved universal primary education. In addition forty percent of eligible secondary school aged students were enrolled in schools. This expansion was the fastest on the continent during the past decade and speaks well for the government's commitment for further development. Although many African countries rapidly expanded their systems after independence, none has attempted universal access to both primary and secondary education to the same extent and as fast as Zimbabwe.

Structure

The policy of educational expansion has involved a massive increase in public expenditure. The government's share of that expansion is managed by a centralized Ministry of Education. Through its four divisions, the Ministry manages the system and controls the curriculum process. However, only 20% of the nation's schools are government owned.   There also is a substantial investment in education by churches, local urban and rural councils, commercial and industrial enterprises and parents. Many non-government schools receive government grants that partially subsidize the cost. Recently new educational regions are being developed to help the Ministry better oversee these private schools.

The educational ladder consists of a 5-year primary cycle followed by a 6-year secondary cycle. The primary level is divided into 3 years lower and 2 years upper. Students who pass the localized leaving examination go to a 4-year basic secondary program which is followed by a 5th and 6th year for those seeking higher education. In an attempt to translate policy into action the government developed experimental socialist schools. Called Zimbabwe Foundation for Education and Production schools, they are designed to engage students in productive agricultural activities.

The University of Zimbabwe is the only degree conferring institution of higher education in the country. It offers degree and post degree courses through six faculties that include the arts, education, engineering, medicine, science and social studies.

Function

The curriculum is managed by the Ministry's Curriculum Development Unit which is responsible for infusing a strong scientific socialist understanding of Zimbabwean society. This is being developed through a curriculum that is oriented toward "education for production" programs that emphasize egalitarian and socialist principles. Toward this end a common curriculum is provided through the first two years of secondary school regardless of ability or location. Since 1986, the curriculum includes required subjects in vocational subjects. The government is attempting to introduce a new syllabus called "The Political Economy of Zimbabwe." The course is to emphasize scientific socialism and the nation's guiding ideology of a Marxist-Leninist perspective. The course ran into opposition from church leaders who view the content as anti-God and anti-religion. Presently the course has been withdrawn and is under revision. English is the official language and the principal medium of instruction. In addition, all government schools teach at least one of the two major African languages. Some rural schools use the local vernacular in the early primary grades.

The rapid expansion of education has caused concern for quality. Most secondary schools are not government owned. Many are day schools and some operate on two shifts. Many lack teaching material and qualified teachers. There also is concern that the urban based private schools could become elitist. In spite of these problems the expanding opportunities have provided a new generation of students with hope for a bright future. With political stability and continued economic development the future could be bright.

BIBLIOGRAPHY

Aluko, Olajide and Timothy Shaw, eds. *Southern Africa in the 1980's*. London: George Allen and Unwin (Publishers) Ltd., 1985.

Barnes, Barbara. "Education for Socialism in Mozambique," in *Comparative Education Review*. Vol.26, No.3, October, 1982, pp. 406-419.

Cameron, John, ed. *International Handbook of Educational Systems*, Volume II. Chichester: John Wiley and Sons, 1983.

Dorsey, Betty Jo. "Educational Development and Reform in Zimbabwe," in *Comparative Education Review*, Vol. 33, No. 1, February, 1989, pp. 40-58.

Fafunwa, A. Babs and J.U. Aisiku, eds. *Education in Africa: A Comparative Survey*. London: George Allen and Unwin, 1982.

Faraj, Abdulatif Hussein. *International Yearbook of Education*, Volume XL-1988. Paris: UNESCO, 1988.

Hawes, Hugh. *Curriculum and Reality in African Primary Schools*. Burnt Mill: Longman Group Ltd., 1979.

Husen, Torsten and T. Neville Postlethwaite, eds. *The International Encyclopedia of Education*. Oxford: Pergamon Press Ltd., 1985.

Jansen, Jonathan. "The State and Curriculum in the Transition to Socialism: The Zimbabwean Experience," in *Comparative Education Review*, Vol. 35, No. 1, February, 1991, pp. 76-91.

July, Robert W. *A History of the African People*. New York: Charles Scribner's Sons, 1974.

Kurian, George T., ed. *World Education Encyclopedia*. New York: Facts on File Publications, 1988.

Mwanakatwe, J.M. *The Growth of Education in Zambia Since Independence*. Lusaka: Oxford University Press, 1968.

Rose, Brian, ed. *Education in Southern Africa*. London: Collier-Macmillan Publishers, 1970.

University of Massachusetts. *Strategies for Supporting Development in Namibia*. Amherst: Center for International Education, 1990.

Wiley, David and Allen Isaacman, eds. *Southern Africa: Society, Economy, and Liberation*. East Lansing: Michigan State University, 1981.

World Bank. *Education in Sub-Saharan Africa*. Washington, D.C.: The World Bank, 1988.

ANNOTATED BIBLIOGRAPHY

History and Philosophy

Books

324. Atkinson, Norman. *Teaching Rhodesians: A History of Educational Policy in Rhodesia.* London: Longman Group Ltd, 1972.

Traces the development of education in a multiracial society and analyzes the political, social and economic influences that affect its development. Describes the unsuccessful attempts made to break down segregation in secondary education and the successful attempts to do so in higher and adult education. Carefully researched with a strong analytical component.

325. Mugomba, Agrippah and Mougo Nyaggah, eds. *Independence Without Freedom: The Political Economy of Colonial Education in Southern Africa.* Santa Barbara: ABC-Clio, Inc., 1980.

Chapters in the book were first presented at an International Conference on Colonial Education and Contemporary Conflict in Southern Africa held at the Santa Barbara campus of the University of California in 1977. Both African and Western authors offer a regional and comparative perspective on the effects of colonial education. In particular, many of the authors discuss how colonial governments separated education from the overall socio-economic development of the people.

326. Samuels, Michael A. *Education in Angola, 1908-1914: A History of Cultural Transfer and Administration.* New York: Teachers College Press, 1970.

Carefully documented history of early formal educational development in Angola. A great deal of attention is given to Christian missionary education. The author uses education as a means of highlighting social and political forces at work during a significant period in colonial history.

327. Snelson, Peter Dormond. *Educational Development in Northern Rhodesia, 1883-1945.* Lusaka: NECZAM, 1974.

Investigates the origins and development of both African and European education. The author discusses the educational activities of missionaries, the British South Africa Company and the colonial government. Good use is made of official publications, and missionary and government archives. Identifies the successes and most prominent failures of the educational policy.

Education and Development

Books

328. Agrel, J.O., I. Fagerlind and I. Gustafsson. *Education and Training in Botswana, 1975-1980.* Stockholm: Swedish International Development Authority, 1982.

Reviews educational programs sponsored by the Swedish government. Offers a frank appraisal of what has been and has not been achieved.

329. Buckland, Peter. *Educational Policy and Reform in Southern Africa.* Cape Town: University of Cape Town, 1983.

330. Chung, Fay and Emmanuel Ngara. *Socialism, Education and Development: A Challenge to Zimbabwe.* Harare: Zimbabwe Publishing House, 1985.

Mr. Chung is presently Minister of Primary and Secondary Education. Prior to his involvement in politics he was an educator for over 20 years. The book discusses his personal philosophy and what education can contribute to development.

331. Crowder, Michael. *Education For Development in Botswana.* Gaborone: Macmillan Botswana Publishing Co., Ltd, 1984.

Proceedings of a symposium held by the Botswana Society in Gaborone during August, 1983. Sections are devoted to education for social justice, rural development, cultural identity and employment. Problems and prospectus for the future also are discussed. Virtually all of the authors reside in Botswana, with the majority of them being indigenous to the country. Good descriptive and statistical information.

332. Fagerlind, I. and J. Valdelin. *Education in Zambia: Past Achievements and Future Trends.* Stockholm: Swedish International Development Authority, 1983.

333. Government of Botswana. *Education For Kagisano: Report on the National Commission on Education.* Gaborone: Government Printer, 1977.

Contains a series of ten studies prepared for the National Commission in connection with an overall assessment of Botswana's educational system. The studies range from an evaluative survey of primary and secondary education, undertaken by Torsten Husen, to the reports of task forces on the curriculum in primary and secondary schools. Also included is the 1976 report on the First National Conference on Nonformal Education and a Bibliography on Education in Botswana and Related Fields. The bibliography contains many of the smaller reports published by the Government Printer.

334. Johnston, A. *Education in Mozambique 1975-1984*. Stockholm: Swedish International Development Authority, 1984.

Prepared by the Education Division as a document which describes and analyzes educational programs sponsored by the Swedish International Development Authority.

335. Kumbula, Tendayi J. *Education and Social Control in Southern Rhodesia*. Palo Alto: R. and E. Research Associates, Inc., 1979.

Evolved out of doctoral dissertation research. Chapters are devoted to the development of primary, secondary and higher education for Africans in a country controlled by a white minority. The political control of education is examined. The book is more of an overview than a detailed account; long on description and short on analysis.

336. Makulu, Henry F. *Education, Development and Nation-Building in Independent Africa: A Study of the New Trends and Recent Philosophy of Education*. London: SCM Press, 1971.

The author was a prominent Zambian churchman and educator. References are most often to education in that country. After discussing colonial and missionary attitudes toward education, he focuses on the present goals and relates them to manpower development. The foreword is contributed by Dr. Kenneth Kaunda, President of Zambia.

337. Mungazi, Dickson A. *The Underdevelopment of African Education: A Black Zimbabwean Perspective*. Washington, D.C.: University Press of America, Inc., 1982.

Describes the problems that have retarded the development of formal education in Africa during and after the colonial period. Highlights the denial of educational opportunity. Devotes one section to African students on campus in the United States. The author wrote the book while a graduate student in the U.S. Personal experiences, and those of his fellow African students, help to enrich the book.

338. Murphree, M.W., ed. *Education, Race and Employment in Rhodesia.* Salisbury, Rhodesia: Artca Publications, 1975.

The book is a result of the Round Table Project on Race Relations established in 1969 and was written by a project team. It highlights the development and utilization of human resources and the fulfillment of human aspirations. Each chapter is carefully researched with data often expressed in tables and graphs. The summary and recommendations are written by the editor and include the major research findings of the study.

339. Mwanakatwe, J.M. *The Growth of Education in Zambia Since Independence.* Lusaka: Oxford University Press, 1974.

Describes the acceleration of educational opportunity since independence and discusses the problems associated with it. The author was the first Minister of Education and his particular perspective is that of a concerned educational leader. Chapters include those related to the problem of language, discipline, training and citizenship, and desegregation of the schools. He provides an analysis of development in education at all levels since independence. A good source book.

340. Rose, Brian., ed. *Education In Southern Africa.* London: Collier-Macmillan, 1970.

Contains chapters that depict educational concerns and problems in the nine countries which make up Southern Africa. The educational concerns are placed within a social, historical and economic context. The book is primarily for students of education in Southern Africa who are studying to be teachers.

341. Sembajwe, Israel. *The Impact of Rapid Population Growth on School Enrollments in Southern Africa.* Roma, Lesotho: National University of Lesotho, 1985.

Articles

342. Barnes, Barbara. "Education for Socialism in Mozambique." *Comparative Education Review* 26, No. 3 (1982): 406-19.

Traces the dramatic educational change that took place in the late

1970's. Within a month after independence schools were nationalized and the majority of teachers who were Portuguese left. The new leaders wanted to use education to produce the "New Man" and a "new mentality." A democratic structure was established in the schools and education became the instrument for social transformation. During the first five years after independence there was a threefold increase in school enrollment. A good overview of an attempt to transform and revolutionize a nation through education.

343.   Dorsey, Betty Jo. "Educational Development and Reform in Zimbabwe." *Comparative Eduction Review* 33, No. 1 (1989): 40-58.

The author is a senior lecturer at the University of Zimbabwe. The article discusses whether mass education can provide equality of opportunity leading to a more egalitarian society, or whether the policy will produce a class-like structure that replaces the racially structured society of the colonial period. She concludes that the potential is there for the development of a more egalitarian society. Carefully researched.

344.   Gillespie, Roselyn R. and Colin Collins.   "Education in Zimbabwe." *Education and Society* 3, No. 1 (1986): 62-68.

345.   Plank, David N. "School Administration and School Reform in Botswana." *International Journal of Educational Development* 7, No. 2 (1987): 119-26.

346.   Lulat, Y.G.M. "Political Constraints on Educational Reform for Development: Lessons from an African Experience." *Comparative Education Review* 26, No. 2 (1982): 235-53.

Highlights the Zambian educational reform effort in the mid-1970's and explains why it did not go very far. Concludes that the proposed reform tampered with the middle class reproduction function of the system. The ideology of Zambian Humanism, with its call to socialism, appeared not to be in the best interests of those in dominant power positions.

Primary Education

Book

347.   Hoppers, Wim H.M.L. *Education in a Rural Society: Primary Pupils and School Leavers in Mwinilunga, Zambia*. The Hague, Netherlands: Centre for the Study of Education in Developing

Countries, 1981.

Article

348. Chung, Fay. "Policies for Primary and Secondary Education in Zimbabwe." *Zimbabwe Journal of Educational Research* 1, No. 1 (1989): 22-42.

Mr. Chung is Minister of Primary and Secondary Education in Zimbabwe. The article is an interview with him in which he gives his perspective on the recent World Bank report on education in Sub-Saharan Africa and relates it to Zimbabwe. Mr. Chung has been involved in African education for over 20 years. His insights offer thoughtful reflections and future prospects for education.

Secondary Education

Books

349. Hurrell, Kathryn E. *Job Opportunities for Secondary School Leavers in Zimbabwe.* Salisbury, Zimbabwe: Centre for Applied Social Sciences, University of Zimbabwe, 1981.

350. Kann, Ulla. *Career Development in a Changing Society: The Case of Botswana.* Stockholm: Institute of International Education, University of Stockholm, 1981.

Traces an interdisciplinary, longitudinal, dissertation study that was carried out among 339 secondary school students. Data include information from questionnaires, achievement and ability tests, examinations and published materials. Findings focus on the influence of societal groups and individual factors on educational achievement and career development. The study found that the single most important determinant of career development in Bostwana was educational achievement.

351. Mehra, A.N. *The Development and Cost of Secondary Education in Relation to Manpower Policy in Zambia.* Lusaka: Institute for African Studies, University of Zambia, 1980.

352. Scudder, Thayer and Elizabeth Colson. *Secondary Education and the Formation of An Elite: The Impact of Education on Gwembe District, Zambia.* London: Academic Press Ltd., 1980.

Describes and analyzes a long-term field research project supported by the Institute of African Studies, University of Zambia. The study is primarily about the first 500 Gwembe Tonga to obtain a post-primary education as full-time boarders at a Zambia secondary school. It assesses the impact of this education on the individuals as well as on the social order of their home district. The effects of an emerging elite, created through formal education, is highlighted.

Tertiary and Higher Education

Books

353. Bardouille, R. *University of Zambia Students' Career Expectations*. Lusaka: Institute for African Studies, University of Zambia, 1981.

354. Mwanalushi, Muyunda. *Youth and Society in Zambia: A Sense of Community Among University Students*. Lusaka: Department of Psychology, University of Zambia, 1983.

355. Sanyal, Bikas C., John H. Case, Philip S. Dow and Mary E. Jackman. *Higher Education and the Labour Market In Zambia: Expectations and Performance*. Paris: UNESCO Press, 1976.

Details a research project directed by Bikas Sanyal at the International Institute for Educational Planning, UNESCO. It is one in a series that analyzes the relationship between education and development. Through the use of a carefully designed methodology, the authors attempt to provide a systematic exploration of select dimensions which link higher education and the labor market. Detailed with tables and graphs.

Specialized Education (Adult, Community, Nonformal, Technical, Vocational)

Books

356. Setsabi, Anthony M., ed. *Development Through Adult Education: Views From Antigonish and Boleswa*. Maseru: National University of Lesotho, 1985.

Contains papers delivered at a conference in Lesotho organized by the Institute of Extra-Mural Studies of the National University of Lesotho. Community development and alternative strategies are the major themes discussed. One section of the book contains practical approaches to common problems. Lesotho is used as a case study for integrating rural development through nonformal education.

357. Setsabi, Anthony M. *Non-formal Education and Training for Productivity and Self-Reliance in Lesotho.* Roma: Institute of Extra Mural Studies, National University of Lesotho, 1984.

A thirty-two page publication prepared initially for the Fifth Biennial Conference of the African Association for Training and Development held in Addis Ababa in November of 1984.

358. Matshazi, Meshack Jonilanga and Christina Tillfors. *A Survey of Workers' Education Activities in Zimbabwe, 1980-1981.* Uppsala: Scandinavian Institute of African Studies, 1983.

359. Treydte, Klaus Peter, Solomon Inguai, Joyce Morris, and Bernhard Weimer. *Survey on Non-Formal Education in Botswana.* Gaborone: University of Botswana, Lesotho and Swaziland, 1976.

Describes the outcome of a survey to provide information for the Rural Extension Coordinating Committee, the University's Division of Extra-Mural Services and the National Education Commission. The team of researchers collected and processed written material and sought new data through field work.

360. van Rensburg, Patrick. *The Serowe Brigades: Alternative Education in Botswana.* London: Macmillan Education Ltd., 1978.

Highlights the growth and function of the Brigades authored by the person who developed them. The book focuses on the Brigades as both productive enterprises and centers of skill training and education. The levels of training are discussed as well as the curriculum and methodology used in developing twenty different skills. A special chapter discusses the factors which influence replicability in other parts of the world.

361. Weimer, Bernhard., ed. *Approaches to Non-Formal Education Training: Botswana Case Studies.* Gaborone: University of Botswana and Swaziland, 1977.

Includes four articles that describe nonformal educational activities related to training. An emphasis is placed on the structure of training with details of specific exercises included. Highlighted is the use of simulation training exercises.

Articles

362.   Hoppers, Wim. "Faces of Innovation: Education, Training and Production in African Youth Programmes." *Education with Production* 5, No. 1 (1986): 8-28.

Comments on ways in which education and training have been allied with production through various institutional formats. Reviews the principles that relate to the alliances. The review is limited to developments in Southern and East Africa.

363.   Mutava, Dominic M. "Training Trade Union Workers in Zambia." *Convergence* 18, Nos. 3-4 (1985): 133-36.

364.   Ota, Cleaver Chakawuya. "Community Financing of Schools in Zimbabwe." *Prospects* 16, No. 3 (1986): 355-68.

Assesses community financing of state and private schools in Zimbabwe. Reviews the historical influences of financing and lists contemporary efforts to redress past injustices.

Curriculum and Methods

Books

365.   Chimuka, S.S., M.E. Kashoki, H.P. Africa, R. Serpell. *Language and Education in Zambia*. Lusaka: Institute for African Studies, University of Zambia, 1978.

Contains four articles by the four authors entitled, "Problems in the administration and staffing of language programmes in Zambia," "Language selection and zoning; Some national implications," "Selection of language modes," and "Learning to say it better: A challenge for Zambian education."

366.   Schorn, Frank and Arthur Blair, eds. *Perspectives on Curriculum and Instruction: Teaching in Lesotho*. Maseru, Lesotho: Morija Press, 1982.

Developed for instructional use by a UNESCO supported teacher education project located at the National University of Lesotho. It also was to be used for general education courses in teacher training programs. Topics include contemporary educational issues, instructional improvement, teacher training and supervision.

Articles

367.   Csapo, Marg. "Special Educational Developments in Zambia."

International Journal of Educational Development 7, No. 2 (1987): 107-12.

368. Csapo, Marg. "Zimbabwe: Emerging Problems of Education and Special Education." *International Journal of Special Education* 1, No. 2 (1986): 141-60.

States that handicapped children are receiving very little special education, and there does not appear to be any national policy to address it. However, the Swedish International Development Agency, in cooperation with the Ministry of Education, recently conducted a national disability survey.

369. Mulopo, Moses and Seymour H. Fowler. "Effects of Traditional and Discovery Instructional Approaches on Learning Outcomes for Learners of Different Intellectual Development: A Study of Chemistry Students in Zambia." *Journal of Research in Science Teaching* 24, No. 3 (1987): 217-27.

Examines a study that reviews the differing effects of traditional and discovery methods on the teaching of chemistry. Comparisons are made in the teaching of science concepts, understandings about science, and scientific attitudes to learners at the concrete and formal levels of cognitive development.

Teachers

Books

370. Stannard, David. *Secondary Level Teachers: Supply and Demand in Zambia*. East Lansing: International Studies in Education and the African Studies Center, Michigan State University, 1970.

Attempts to determine the demand for expatriate teachers in the secondary schools. The study is no longer relevant, but the analysis of the reasons why expatriate teachers were necessary during this period reveals colonial thinking about the development of secondary education.

Articles

371. Chivore, B.R.S. "Form IV Pupils' Perception of and Attitudes Toward the Teaching Profession in Zimbabwe." *Comparative Education* 22, No. 3 (1986): 233-53.

Surveys 577 secondary students to determine attitudes toward teaching as a profession. The profession in general, and secondary teaching in particular, was more attractive to women, students from rural schools, and pupils whose parents had low academic qualifications.

372. Davies, Lynn. "Contradictions of Control: Lessons from Exploring Teachers' Work in Botswana." *International Journal of Educational Development* 8, No. 4 (1988): 293-304.

Religion and Private Education

Books

373. Ragsdale, John P. *Protestant Mission Education in Zambia, 1880-1954.* Selinsgrove, PA: Susquehanna University Press, 1986.

Article

374. Kaluba, L.H. "Education in Zambia: The Problem of Access to Schooling and the Paradox of the Private Solution." *Comparative Education* 22, No. 2 (1986): 159-70.

Education for Women

Book

375. UNICEF. *Children and Women in Zambia: A Situation Analysis.* Lusaka: UNICEF, 1979.

A survey conducted jointly by UNICEF and the government of Zambia to determine present and future needs in the fields of health, education and social facilities. Also examines the government's policy in development in these three areas and the administrative structure designed to implement the policy.

Article

376. Dorsey, Betty Jo. "Women in the Academic World in Zimbabwe." *Zimbabwe Journal of Educational Research* 1, No. 1 (1989): 119-22.

Describes the current situation of under-representation of women in all faculties at the University of Zimbabwe. Outlines a research project that will focus on the career opportunities and job satisfaction of women at the University. Dr. Dorsey, a senior lecturer at the University, heads a three-person team conducting the major study.

SOUTH AFRICA

Introduction

The independence and self-rule that has come to the Black majority in Sub-Saharan Africa did not reach the nation that occupies the southern part of the continent. Here, white minority rule continues to exist and the demand for "one man-one vote" is far from becoming a reality. As the nation moves into the last decade of the twentieth century sweeping social and political changes are occurring. Laws that strictly segregate the Black and white communities have been overturned and political leaders in both societies have begun to talk of cooperation if not integration. Yet there is little doubt that white supremacy remains the rule of the land and Black South Africans continue to be denied even the semblance of equal educational opportunity in their native land.

Educational inequality has a long history in South Africa. It can be traced from 1948 when the National Party came to power. The leadership of the party solidified through law what already had been put into place by the white minority. This was the system of social and economic privilege for whites with absolute control of the government. The new laws led to the policy of "apartheid" which separated the races and classified all South Africans into four population registration groups: African, Coloured, Indian, and White.

The developers of "apartheid" argued that the separation of the races would allow each society to develop on its own independently and thus prosper and become self-sufficient. Over the years the white minority government put that policy into operation. Ten African homelands or Bantustans were formed. Each was to have its own government, public services, schools and universities. Thirteen percent of the land, much of it not arable, was given to the African homelands while the other 87% was reserved for the white minority. By 1990 three of the homelands were declared independent. In reality all of the African homelands became a series of dependent satellites under the strict control of the minority government. Under the guise of self-rule Africans were being placed in subservience where, in order to survive economically, they were dependent upon the white minority political structure. The homelands also tended to separate the Africans by ethnic or tribal groups and thus developed suspicion and competition for limited economic resources.

From the beginning the policy of total apartheid was seen as unworkable if the white minority were going to have access to cheap

African labor.   The expanding mining and industrial complexes needed to tap into the large reserve of African labor.   As a consequence a series of "temporary" residences were established around the major urban areas where those workers could reside. Eventually one-third of all Africans moved to these segregated urban areas where the majority lived in poor housing and received wages that keep them below the poverty line.

The apartheid laws that emerged in the 1950's included a series of educational provisions that established separate systems for the education of the four groups.   The Bantu Education Act of 1953 was the capstone for the education of Africans.   It dictated central government control and formed the Division of Bantu Education within the Department of Native Affairs.   By the 1960's Bantu Education had its own department and its goals were clear. Education for Africans was to prepare the youth for life in a totally separate community.   The medium of instruction was to be in the local vernacular, special attention was to be paid to Bantu culture, and the subject matter was to prepare the youth for vocations found in the rural Bantustans.   Special higher educational institutions, including universities, were to be established that would prepare a small group of Africans for service and leadership roles in their own community.

The failure of Bantu education to prepare the youth for a role in a modern society is well documented.   Education in a local language did not prepare students to cope with a modern scientific and technological world.   It also limited communication and cohesion with different ethnic groups.   The rigid regulations imposed on all levels of education stifled initiative and development and ensured that the African would remain subservient to the ruling white minority.

Some reform in Bantu education has occurred.   The 1981 deLange Committee Report on Education in South Africa eventually led to more funds being devoted to the education of Africans. Provisions also were made for better teacher education, the expansion of secondary education and the use of English and Afrikaans as mediums of instruction.   A Department of Education and Training was developed which assumed administrative responsibility in those areas that are not homelands and special attention was paid to the urban Africans, especially after the Soweto riots of 1976.   However, these reforms were always within the context of a racially segregated society.

Recently, widespread African protests and the rise of political power groups have caused the apartheid walls to shake, but not tumble. Reform has included the evolution of more co-racial public schools and universities as well as some curriculum revisions. However, it is difficult to predict whether the pace of reform is quick enough to prevent a revolution.

Overview

Several major factors affect education in South Africa, but none greater than race and its relationship to political power. The nation has four distinct educational systems each with its own characteristics. They serve the "African, Coloured, Indian, and White" populations. These separate and apartheid systems show clear inequities and create hostilities that reverberate world wide and affect any discussion of education.

A second factor is the nation's rapid movement toward urbanization and industrialization. Over 70% of the nation's gross national product now comes from its industrial base. This has helped to produce a dramatic growth in four urban centers where over one-third of all Africans live and where well over 75% of all Asians and Coloured, and 88% of all Whites reside. This movement has implications for education that go beyond sheer numbers. The need to develop a better African educated work force is beginning to be recognized.

Another important factor is the movement by Africans, often forced, to the ten designated homelands, three classified as "independent" and seven as "nonindependent." The African leadership in these homelands are expected to develop their own departments of education most often with limited resources.

The difficulty of reporting on education in a nation that is involved in turmoil and apparent social change is another factor that must be considered. Whether the apartheid systems of education will remain as they are or evolve into something different is a matter that is being discussed and debated at length. What is obvious is that the white minority government will have a difficult time maintaining the status quo where a majority of the financial resources go toward the education of the white population.

Structure

The apartheid systems have produced a complex administrative structure that is difficult to describe. Since 1970 there has been a

Department of National Education that presently oversees all formal education for whites in the Republic. This includes the four provincial departments for white education that manage through regional offices. However, the four provinces retain their own independence within the framework of national policy. All higher education, regardless of race, falls within the jurisdiction of the Department of National Education.

For those Africans who live in the homelands, education is administered by their own respective departments of education. For those outside these territories the management of education is through the Department of Education and Training where the education for Africans is referred to as "Bantu Education." This department exercises control over all schools excluding the universities. They also serve as a central liaison and advisor to the departments located in the homelands as well as provide some financial assistance. The senior education officers located at the headquarters of the department are primarily white.

The management of "Coloured" education falls under the jurisdiction of the Administration of Coloured Affairs where the Commissioner works through a Director of Education. Asian education is centrally controlled through the Minister of Indian Affairs, who also has a Director of Education.

There are a growing number of churches and voluntary bodies that provide education for all ethnic groups, but the majority of these are for the white population. Some of these private institutions receive state aid.

The educational ladder for all systems consists of four phases, each three years in length: junior and senior primary, and junior and senior secondary. For Africans, promotion from one grade to the next is not automatic, but depends upon the pupil reaching a satisfactory level of achievement. However, most students are promoted according to age. African students take an external examination at the end of the senior primary cycle to determine whether they continue education at the secondary level. White students also are expected to make satisfactory progress from one grade to the next. The first external examination takes place at the end of senior secondary school and determines access to higher education.

While the educational ladder is the same for all four systems there is a vast difference in the teacher-pupil ratio, the qualifications of teachers, the quality of the buildings and the amount of expenditure per pupil. During the past few years considerable amounts of money have been spent to up-grade the education of African, Asian and Coloured children. However, the many years of neglect have made it difficult to overcome all the obstacles.

Adding to the neglect of education for Africans is the condition of the farm schools where approximately 25% of all students are enrolled. These schools are located out of the urban areas and homelands. They are found on the land of white farmers and are financed by the farmers and the Department of Education and Training. Most have limited levels of schooling and few opportunities for school leavers outside of staying in the employment of the white farmers. Farmers have the right to close down the schools at their discretion.

All universities are financed by the state. The University of South Africa is the largest and enrolls students from all ethnic groups. It is mainly a correspondence university and functions in both official languages -- Afrikaans and English. Most universities reserved for whites are either Afrikaans or English speaking. The most renowned university for African students is the University of Fort Hare founded in 1916 as a "native college." In addition there are seven universities for Africans located among the major African ethnic groups such as the Xhosa and Zulu people. Some homelands have developed their own universities. The "Coloured" community has its own university and so does the "Indian" community. During the past decade there has been an easing of racial restrictions and many of the white institutions now serve all racial groups.

Function

In theory, the curriculum in the schools of all four ethnic groups is the same. However, in practice white pupils have much better trained teachers, lower pupil-teacher ratios and their schools are predominately academic in their orientation. Much more emphasis is placed on vocational and technical schooling for the three other groups. The drop out rate for African students at the primary level is very high. Many leave school after the first two years. It is estimated that approximately half of the African population is illiterate. For whites, schooling is in either Afrikaans or English. The breakdown is about 60% Afrikaans and 40% English. After the lower primary cycle all ethnic groups take their examinations in either Afrikaans or English. Recent attempts to move African students toward a greater use of Afrikaans in the schools led to rioting and the closing of schools.

It is difficult to predict future trends in education in a nation that is in the middle of rapid social and political change. More schools now enroll all four ethnic groups; however, these are the exception. Whether that trend will continue is difficult to foresee. Education at all levels is dominated by Afrikaners, both administratively and in the teaching force. At present only a few see the need to improve the education of all citizens in order to produce a more knowledgeable and better skilled workforce.

The rest of Africa, and many parts of the world, are anxiously watching South Africa, the last bastion of a white minority government on the continent, as it attempts to control the increasingly restless African youth. A peaceful solution might not prove possible.

BIBLIOGRAPHY

Aluko, Olajide and Timothy Shaw, eds. *Southern Africa in the 1980's.* London: George Allen and Unwin (Publishers) Ltd., 1985.

Behr, A.L. *Perspectives in South African Education.* Durban: Butterworths, 1978.

Christie, Pam. *The Right to Learn: The Struggle for Education in South Africa.* Braamfontein: Ravan Press (Pty) Ltd., 1985.

Christie, Pam and Margaret Gaganakis. "Farm Schools in South Africa: The Face of Rural Apartheid," in *Comparative Education Review*, Vol. 33, No. 1, February, 1989, pp. 77-92.

Geber, Beryl and Stanton Newman. *Soweto's Children: The Development of Attitudes.* London: Academic Press Inc., 1980.

Husen, Torsten and T. Neville Postlethwaite, eds. *The International Encyclopedia of Education.* Oxford: Pergamon Press Ltd., 1985.

Kurian, George T., ed. *World Education Encyclopedia.* New York: Facts on File Publication, 1988.

Marcum, John A. *Education, Race and Social Change in South Africa.* Berkeley: University of California Press, 1982.

Nkomo, Mokubung, ed. *Pedagogy of Domination: Toward a*

Democratic Education in South Africa. Trenton: Africa World Press, Inc., 1991.

Wiley, David and Allen Isaacman, eds. *Southern Africa: Society, Economy, and Liberation*. East Lansing: Michigan State University, 1981.

ANNOTATED BIBLIOGRAPHY

History and Philosophy

Books

377. Behr, A.L., ed. *A New Educational Dispensation for the Republic of South Africa.* Pretoria: The South African Association for the Advancement of Education, 1985.

Contains the papers read at the Twenty-Fourth Congress of the South African Association for the Advancement of Education held in January, 1985. The authors reflect different viewpoints on how educational reform is to be accomplished. The majority of the papers are in Afrikan with the remaining in English. Those written in English are very basic and primarily descriptive. They do not address the issue of apartheid.

378. Bozzoli, G.R. *Education is the Key to Change in South Africa.* Pietermaritzburg: Natal Witness Ltd., 1977.

Consists of the Alfred and Winifred Hoernle Memorial Lecture for 1977 delivered by the Vice-Chancellor and Principal of the University of Witwatersrand. The annual lecture is given under the auspices of the South African Institute of Race Relations. The author denigrates segregated universities and discusses the social and educational implications of such institutions. He calls for universities open to all.

379. Christie, Pam. *The Right to Learn: The Struggle for Education in South Africa.* Braamfontein, South Africa: Ravan Press, 1985.

The author intends the book to be a contribution to the on-going debate over education. It does not attempt to be neutral, but rather presents a particular point of view that emphasizes the struggle for education under apartheid. Chapters discuss such topics as the hidden curriculum, the church and education and resistance in education. The book contains illustrations that help to present a particular viewpoint.

380. February, V.A. *From the Arsenal: The Teachers' League of South Africa: A Documentary Study of "Coloured" Attitudes Between 1913-1980.* Leiden, Netherlands: African Studies Centre, 1983.

381. Luthuli, P.C. *The Philosophical Foundations of Black Education in South Africa*. Woburn, MA: Butterworths, 1981.

382. Luthuli, P.C. *An Introduction to Black-oriented Education in South Africa*. Woburn, MA: Butterworths, 1982.

383. Pells, E.G. *300 Years of Education in South Africa*. Westport, CT: Greenwood Press, 1970.

An historical account of educational development for white South Africans. Educational leaders are identified as are important government acts and actions. The chapter on "Native Education" is derogatory in the extreme.

384. Perold, Helene and Dawn Butler, eds. *The Right to Learn: The Struggle For Education in South Africa*. Braamfontein: Ravan Press Ltd., 1985.

The book is intended as a contribution to the current debate over education in South Africa. It does not attempt to be neutral since the editors do not believe that is possible. It does attempt to look at crucial issues in education and present ways of understanding them. A straightforward book which presents cogent opinions on topics which range from "what's education about" to "the hidden curriculum" to "resistance in education." Well worth reading.

385. Tabata, I.B. *Education for Barbarism in South Africa*. London: Unity Movement of South Africa, 1980.

Describes Bantu (apartheid) education. The preface is written by Patrick Noube. It was first printed in 1960, and reprinted in 1980.

Articles

386. Cross, Michael. "A Historical Review of Education in South Africa: Towards an Assessment." *Comparative Education* 22, No. 3 (1986): 185-200.

Explores changing attitudes toward the education of Black South Africans through a study of texts and statements by leading white politicians and historians. Reviews dominant schools of educational thought along political lines.

387. Dube, Ernest. "The Relationship between Racism and Education in South Africa." *Harvard Educational Review* 55,

No. 1 (1985): 86-100.

Traces the relationship in light of the racist policies and practices implemented by the government. Discusses the introduction of Bantu education and pays particular attention to the intended and unintended outcomes of the system.

388.   Friedman, Harold and Helen Friedman.   "South Africa." *Integrated Education* 20, No. 6 (1983): 32-35.

Excerpts interviews conducted in South Africa with people in different walks of life to determine the range of opinions on Black education. Assesses the degree to which there is consensus toward equal educational opportunity.

389.   Friedman, Helen and Harold, Friedman. "Black Education in South Africa." *Integrated Education* 21, Nos. 1-6 (1983): 3-92.

Contains a detailed discussion of racial discrimination in the schools through interviews with government officials, political activists, students, teachers, parents and others. Focuses on Black and white protests. The appendix includes an historical perspective on school apartheid.

390.   Hyslop, J. "State Education Policy and the Social Reproduction of the Urban Working Class -- the Case of the Southern Transvaal, 1955-1976." *Journal of Southern African Studies* 14, No. 3 (1988): 446-482.

391.   Reagan, Timothy and Issac Ntshoe.   "Language Policy and Black Education in South Africa." *Journal of Research and Development in Education* 20, No. 2 (1987): 1-8.

Presents an historical overview of the language policy that emerged in African education. The present language policy also is reviewed and an equitable policy proposed.

392.   Reagan, Timothy.   "Language Policy, Politics and Ideology: The Case of South Africa." *Issues in Education* 2, No. 2 (1984): 155-64.

Focuses on the relations between national language policies, ideologies and education. Emphasizes the politics of language usage and relates it to education. Takes into consideration the educational response to cultural and linguistic diversity.

Education and Development

Books

393. Behr, A.L. *New Perspectives in South African Education.*
Durban: Butterworths, 1978.

Utilizes the National Education Policy Act of 1967 as a point of
departure to discuss educational development. The first half of the
book reviews the 1967 Act and other subsequent government acts and
discusses the implications of the government action as it pertains to
the education of whites. The 1967 Act laid down a uniform
educational policy for the education of whites. However, adaptations
of the Act affected the education of Blacks, Coloureds, and Indians.
The second half of the book discusses how the education of these
groups is affected.

394. Blignaut, Sue. *Statistics on Education in South Africa, 1968-79.*
Johannesburg: South African Institute of Race Relations, 1981.

395. Education Department. *The Educational Systems of the
Republic of South Africa.* Pietermaritzburg: University of Natal,
1982.

Contains a report prepared by a working group in the Department of
Education, University of Natal. It was prepared for the Working
Committee on Educational Systems of the Human Sciences Research
Council Investigation Into Education. The report critically analyzes
the state of education for the Committee. It balances descriptive and
statistical information with specific criticisms of both the gap between
policy and practice, and structural and functional deficiencies.

396. Kallaway, Peter, ed. *Apartheid and Education: The Education
of Black South Africans.* Johannesburg: Ravan Press, 1984.

397. Kallaway, Peter, Jackie Kallaway and Deborah Sheward. *A
Bibliography of Education for Black South Africans.*
Rondebosch, South Africa: Department of Education,
University of Cape Town, 1986.

398. Lawrence, Michael, ed. *South African Education Policy:
Analysis and Critique, The Proceedings of the Kenton Conference,
6-9 November, 1981.* Cape Town: Faculty of Education,
University of Cape Town, 1982.

399. South African Association for the Advancement of Education. *Educational Practice in Terms of Educational Policy: An Evaluation.* Papers read at the Eighteenth Congress of the South African Association for the Advancement of Education, held on 15-17 January, 1980. Durban: South African Association for the Advancement of Education, 1980.

400. South Africa, Department of Internal Affairs. *Education for Life: The Education of the Coloured Population Group in the Republic of South Africa: Short History. Present System, Future Perspective.* Cape Town: Department of Internal Affairs, South Africa, 1981.

401. South Africa, Department of National Education. *White Paper on the Provision of Education in the Republic of South Africa.* Pretoria: Government Printer, 1983.

402. Tunmer, Raymond, ed. *The De Lange Report: Assessment and Implementation, the Future of Education in South Africa: Proceedings of the National Education Conference, 4-6 February, 1982.* Grahamstown: 1820 Foundation, 1982.

403. University of Witwatersrand. *South Africa's Crisis in Education.* Johannesburg: University of Witwatersrand, 1978.

The University's Senate appointed a committee to arrange a series of lectures on what they believed was one of the most urgent matters facing South Africa -- that of Black education. The lecture series, published here, was triggered by the Soweto disturbances of 1976 when the youth, through protests and rioting, expressed dissatisfaction with their educational system. Themes represented in the lectures include politics and education, factors in the conflict over education and identity, culture and curriculum. The lectures were delivered by both Black and white scholars from South Africa.

Articles

404. Chisholm, Linda. "Redefining Skills: Black Education in South Africa in the 1980's." *Comparative Education* 19, No. 3 (1983): 57-71.

Assesses recent South African educational reforms as a response by the government to critics of apartheid.

405. De Lange Report. "The De Lange Report." *Comparative Education Review* 28, No. 4 (1984): 625-38.

The De Lange Report of 1981 is a major educational statement by the government of South Africa. It is the most comprehensive and detailed report prepared by the government and is viewed as part of their total strategic policy. The report poses educational problems as technical and manpower questions.

406. Garvey-Mwazi, Kris. "Namibia." *Integrated Education* 20, No. 6 (1983): 25-28.

Describes education for Blacks and Coloureds in Namibia as a tool of apartheid which endeavors to keep the people illiterate or at best semi-skilled. Also discusses efforts by the United Nations Council for Namibia to provide Namibians with equal educational opportunity.

407. Peteni, R.L. "Black Education in South Africa." *Today's Education* 69, No. 4 (1980): 62-65.

Views educational issues as part of the basic struggle for equality. States that compulsory education and higher education for Blacks must be brought up to the same quality level of education as that for whites in South Africa.

408. Simon, Alan. "Black Students' Perceptions of Factors Related to Academic Performance in a Rural Area of Natal Province, South Africa." *Journal of Negro Education* 55, No. 4 (1986): 535-47.

Asserts that Black education is inferior in every way as a result of apartheid. Explores a 1983-84 study for the reasons behind poor academic performance by Blacks. Students see their performance hindered by the teachers, themselves, the facilities and equipment, unfair marking, poor home conditions and difficulty with the English language.

Primary Education

Article

409. Liddell, Christine. "Some Issues Regarding the Introduction of Preschool Enrichment Programmes for Black South African Children." *International Journal of Educational Development* 7, No. 2 (1987): 127-32.

Secondary Education

Book

410.   Geber, Beryl A. and Stanton P. Newman. *Soweto's Children: The Development of Attitudes*. London: Academic Press, 1980.

Examines the social psychological consequences of being young, educated and Black in a society which is clearly structured on the basis of race. The authors detail the experiences and feelings of students in four Soweto schools after the protests and rioting which took place in June, 1976. Also discusses the results of an earlier study undertaken in the 1960's by the author which identifies the aspirations, expectations and values of 1,000 secondary school students found in four schools in Soweto. Both social psychological studies are worth examining today in light of comparable protests from students in the 1980's.

Article

411.   McKenna, Michael and Angus H. MacLarty.   "Secondary Reading in Black South Africa." *Journal of Reading* 31, No. 1 (1987):   44-49.

States that problems of language, culture, teacher training, economics and social circumstances all affect how secondary school teachers handle reading in content areas.

Tertiary and Higher Education

Books

412.   Marcum, John A. *Education, Race, and Social Change in South Africa*. Berkeley: University of California Press, 1983.

Contains materials gathered by a team of senior American university administrators during a visit to South Africa in 1981. The team was sent by the United States-South Africa Leader Exchange Program, a private multiracial association of American and South Africans. The team concentrated its inquiry on the character, quality and accessibility of South African higher education. The documents presented in the book include lectures, government reports, inaugural addresses and the findings of the American team. A multiracial perspective is evident.

413.   Nkomo, Mokubung O. *Student Culture and Activism in Black South African Universities: The Roots of Resistance*. Westport, CT: Greenwood Press, 1984.

414.   Thembela, A.J., ed. *A University on an African Soil: Toward a Definition of Goals*. Kwa Dlangezwa: University of Zululand, 1982.

Highlights the proceedings of a symposium held in 1981 at the University of Zululand to help clarify the goals of the institution. To help in the process a series of speakers describe what has been accomplished in the first 22 years of the University's existence and suggest what needs to be accomplished in the future. The speakers were aware of the political and academic controversy that surrounds the institution.

415.   van der Merwe, H.W. and David Welsh, eds. *The Future of the University in Southern Africa*. Epping Cape, South Africa: Printpax Cape Ltd., 1977.

Provides the proceedings of a 1976 Conference sponsored by the Centre for Intergroup Studies and the University of Cape Town. The Conference brought together senior academics and administrators to discuss issues that affect universities throughout Southern Africa. A comparative perspective can be found in the first three chapters which review the role of American universities. This is followed by a general discussion of the role of the university in nation-building and case studies of the Universities of Rhodesia and Malawi. However, the bulk of the book discusses the role of South African universities in a divided society.

Articles

416.   *Chronicle of Higher Education*. "South Africa: The Crisis, The Campuses, and Some Messages for Americans." *Chronicle of Higher Education* 32, No. 15 (1986): 1-20.

Reviews the difficult challenges facing universities including the admission of more Blacks, increased tension, student leaders challenging the principles of white rule and Black universities attempting to deal with Third World problems.

417.   van As, Ben S. "Transitional Study Programmes at the Distance Teaching University of South Africa: A Continuing Experiement." *Distance Education* 6, No. 2 (1985): 223-34.

Examines the high dropout and failure rate at the University. Describes the development of a transitional study program designed to give underprepared students remedial help including course organization and content.

418.   Zeitman, Aletta and Michael Gering. "Admission to University in an Academically Nonhomogeneous Society (South Africa)." *Higher Education* 15, Nos. 1-2 (1986): 25-36.

Specialized Education (Adult, Community, Nonformal, Technical, Vocational)

Books

419.   Behr, A.L., ed. *Non-formal Education: Papers Read at the Twenty-Second Congress of the South African Association for the Advancement of Education held on 19 and 20 January, 1984 at the University of the Orange Free State.* Pretoria: South African Association for the Advancement of Education, 1984.

420.   Junkin, Elizabeth Darby, ed. *South African Passage: Diaries of the Wilderness Leadership School.* Golden, CO: Fulcrum, 1987.

421.   South Africa, President's Council. *Report of the Science Committee of the President's Council on Informal and Non-formal Education in South Africa.* Pretoria: Government Printers, 1984.

Articles

422.   Adler, Jill. "Newspaper-based Mathematics for Adults in South Africa." *Educational Studies in Mathematics* 19, No. 1 (1988): 59-78.

423.   Christie, Pam and Margaret Gaganakis. "Farm Schools in South Africa: The Face of Rural Apartheid." *Comparative Education Review* 33, No. 1 (1989): 77-92.

Farm schools are currently the largest category of African schools in "white" South Africa and their number is increasing. The authors first formulate a theory of farm schooling within the overall government policy and then carefully analyze the system. Their conclusions note the similarity of the schools to Third World rural education with high drop-out rates, low levels of literacy, overcrowding and broken attendance records. They see the conditions that shape farm schools related to the particular form of racial capitalist development found in rural South Africa.

424. Nasson, Bill. "Farm Schools: Bitter Harvest for Black South Africans." *Perspectives in Education* 10, No. 1 (1988): 13-41.

425. Walters, Shirley and Glenda Krus. "People's Education in South Africa." *Convergence* 21, No. 1 (1988): 17-27.

426. Wolfson, J.G.E. "Computer-Based Learning in Adult Education: A South African Case Study." *Programmed Learning and Educational Technology* 23, No. 1 (1986): 76-83.

Describes a project in which PLATO terminals were used to facilitate the education of adult Blacks. The social, economic and political problems of the adult learner are discussed and related to the reasons for using computers. The Project's implementation problems are reviewed.

Curriculum and Methods

Books

427. Beard, P.N.G. and W.E. Morrow. *Problems of Pedagogics: Pedagogics and the Study of Education in South Africa.* Woburn, MA: Butterworths, 1981.

428. Behr, A.L. *Implication for the Science and Practice of Education.* Pretoria: South African Association for the Advancement of Education, University of South Africa, 1981.

429. Brindley, D.J. *South African and African Literature: A Selected Annotated Bibliography: A Guide for Schools, Colleges, and Universities.* Johannesburg: Heinemann Educational Books, 1982.

430. Dean, Elizabeth, Paul Hartmann and May Katzen. *History in Black and White: An Analysis of South African School History Textbooks.* Paris: UNESCO, 1983.

431. Short, Ann. *Seeking Change: Education for the Disadvantaged in South Africa.* Ypsilanti, MI: High/Scope Press, 1985.

Articles

432. Csapo, Margaret. "Separate Development: Education and Special Education in South Africa." *International Journal of Special Education* 1, No. 1 (1986): 49-91.

433. Helm, H. "Misconceptions in Physics Amongst South African Students." *Physics Education* 15, No. 2 (1980): 92-97.

Examines the misconceptions and reviews the physics test administered to select high school and college students.

434. Jansen, Jonathan D. "Curriculum Change and Contextual Realities in South African Education: 'Cui Bono'?" *Journal of Curriculum Studies* 20, No. 6 (1988): 521-527.

Examines and evaluates two projects in relation to the contextual realities of Black schooling. The projects were the Science Education Project, that attempted to improve science teaching through practical work in Black high schools, and the Fort Hare Project, which provided professional preparation for student teachers through practical training in Black high schools. The author concludes that meaningful change cannot be achieved by working within the confines of the state system of education.

435. Lawrence, Michael. "Moral Education or Indoctrination in South Africa? A Brief Response to Potgieter." *Journal of Moral Education* 11, No. 3 (1982): 188-91.

Presents a response to Potgieter's article "Moral Education in South Africa." (Volume 9, No. 2, 1980). Argues that Potgieter ignores the social and economic complexities which often make moral education a form of indoctrination.

436. MacDonald, M. Allyson and John Rogan. "Innovation in South African Science Education: Science Teaching Observed." *Science Education* 72, No. 2 (1988): 225-36.

437. Millar, Clive. "Curriculum Improvement or Social Innovation? A Case Study in Teacher Education at a Black South African University." *Journal of Curriculum Studies* 16, No. 3 (1984): 297-310.

Discusses the development of a new course in teacher education and explains its reasons for failure based on institutional, cultural and political realities.

438. Potgieter, Peter C. "Moral Education in South Africa." *Journal of Moral Education* 9, No. 2 (1980): 130-33.

Notes that moral education permeates the total curriculum especially in social studies and religion. The code of conduct for white teachers is quoted. Different provisions for Black education are described and segregated schooling discussed.

439. Randolph-Robinson, Brenda. "The Depiction of South Africa in Children's Literature." *Interracial Books for Children Bulletin* 15, No. 7-8 (1984): 14-22.

Examines a bibliography of books about South Africa available to American school libraries. Asserts that the literature is inadequate or misleading.

440. Skuy, Mervyn. "Remedial Education in South Africa: Contribution of the Private Sector." *Journal for Special Educators* 19, No. 1 (1982): 69-77.

Collected data from 14 remedial and 208 regular private schools, as well as 180 remedial therapists, on such topics as problems handled, staff qualifications and multiracial practices. Concludes that 42 percent of white and three percent of Black schools offer services to learning disabled children.

Teachers

Article

441. Rogan, J.M. and M.A. MacDonald. "The In-Service Teacher Education Component of an Innovation: A Case Study in an African Setting." *Journal of Curriculum Studies* 17, No. 1 (1985): 63-85.

Examines a science education project aimed at improving the teaching of science. Suggests that the methodology identified as effective in the developed world also was appropriate in developing countries.

Religion and Private Education

Articles

442. Chohan, Ahmed Ayoob. "Muslim Education in South Africa: It's Present Position." *Muslim Education Quarterly* 5, No. 2 (1988): 67-75.

443. Nadvi, Syed Habibul Haq. "A Critical Overview of Muslim Education in South Africa." *Muslim Education Quarterly* 5, No. 2 (1988): 55-66.

AFRICAN CURRICULUM ORGANIZATION

The African Curriculum Organization (ACO) is an association of government, or government recognized, curriculum centers located throughout the continent. It was jointly organized in 1975 by the International Curriculum Organization, UNESCO, The German Foundation for International Development, and the Swedish International Development Authority. In 1976 the Organization was approved and officially declared by the African Ministers of Education. The Secretariat was based in Ibadan, Nigeria.

The ACO views itself as an association of curriculum institutions. It holds conferences attended by members and associates, sends members overseas and undertakes research and development projects. Listed below is a good representation of the studies undertaken under the auspices of the ACO in the 1980's. At times special themes were developed. The titles are occasionally disjointed. All the studies listed were printed in Nairobi, Kenya, by the African Curriculum Organization. Although difficult to obtain, they are worth reviewing.

WEST AFRICA

Ado, Patience A. *The Development of Population Education Curriculum for an Elementary School in Ghana.* 1981.

Ajie, Victor Elemchuku Nwaji. *A Critical Study of In-Service Teacher Education for Primary School Teachers in Rivers State, Nigeria.* 1981.

Akinseloyin, Timothy Oyewole. *A Study of Students' Riots in Secondary Schools in Ondo State of Nigeria.* 1981.

Lamine, Male. *A Study of the Causes and Effects of Pupils Dropout in the Fundamental School Level in Mali.* 1983.

Lemu, Muhammed. *Improving the Number of Qualified Teachers Through In-Service Programme in Niger State of Nigeria via Distance Learning System.* 1981.

Okpe, Godwin U. *The Development of Curriculum Content for Pre-Service Training of Auxiliary Teachers in Anambra State of Nigeria.* 1981.

Samba, Wutama Bulama. *Evaluation of Social Studies Programme in Government Teachers Colleges in Borno State, Nigeria.*

1981.

Sidibe, M. *An Evaluation of Educational Radio Programme for Primary School Teachers in Mali.* 1983.

CENTRAL AFRICA

Anicet, Mawaka. *An Examination of the Structure and Organization of Teaching Practice in Primary Teachers Training Colleges in the People's Republic of the Congo.* 1982.

Bafoua, Justin. *An Examination of Indiscipline in Secondary Schools in the Congo.* 1983.

Kouma, Felix. *A Study of Problems Faced by Teachers in the Congo and Some Practical Solutions.* 1981.

Mombod, Josephine Ntinou. *Developing Models/Techniques in the Teaching of English as a Second Foreign Language in Senior Secondary Schools in the Congo.* 1983.

Ngoma, Jean Jeannot. *The Impact of Rural Adult Education on Socioeconomic Development in the Congo.* 1983.

EAST AFRICA

Ahmed, Mumina M. *Syllabus Outline on Child Care for Day Care Teachers at Family Life Teacher Training Centre in Somalia.* 1983.

Awooter, Dayasingh. *A Study of the Problems Which Have Hindered the Effective Teaching of Physical Education at the Primary Level in Mauritus.* 1983.

Awuor, Mordoch Ouko. *An Examination of Teaching Practice as a Component of Primary Teacher Training in Kenya.* 1982.

Bahar, Ismail F.F. *The Role of National Adult Education Centre in Curriculum Development in Somalia in Selected Government Primary Adult Schools in Mogadisho.* 1983.

Ciano, J. *Causes and Effects of Secondary School Drop-Out in Nairobi, Kenya.* 1983.

Dirie, Mohamed Farah. *Handwriting Manual for Primary Teachers in Somalia.* 1982.

Ferede, Yigzaw. *The Role of Elementary School Teachers in Curriculum Development and Implementation in Selected Government Elementary Schools of Addis Ababa.* 1981.

Gaber, Haile H. *Contribution of Arwaja Pedagogical Centers to the Improvement of Education in Ethiopia.* 1980.

Gicheri, K. *An Investigation of the Factors That Adversely Affect the Teaching of French in Kenya Secondary Schools.* 1983.

Good, Mahamed Farah Ahmed. *The Role of Primary School Teachers in Curriculum Development and Implementation in Selected Government Primary Schools of Mogadisho.* 1982.

Isengwa, I.P. *An Evaluation of the Teacher Training Programme of Agricultural Teachers for Secondary Schools in Tanzania.* 1983.

Jama, Mohamed A.F. *Evaluation of Mathematics Curriculum in Primary Teacher Training Institute in Somalia.* 1983.

Katigula, Barnabas A.J. *Towards Determining Learning Activities of Pre-School Education in Tanzania.* 1981.

Kiigi, Evans. *An Examination of History Teaching in Kenya Secondary Schools.* 1983.

Kirui, Kipngetich. *A Study of the Factors that Influence the Increasing Repetition and Drop-out Rates in Primary Schools in Nandi District of Kenya.* 1982.

Madeje, B.V. *Evaluation of the Implementation of the Physical Education Program in Dar es Salaam City Primary Schools.* 1981.

Masagara, E.M. *The Role of Teacher Advisory Centres in the Education of Teachers in Kenya: A Case Study of Nandi District.* 1983.

Masota, Laurent Anatoly. *Investigation of the Effectiveness of Teacher Education Curriculum in Primary School Mathematics on Tanzania Mainland.* 1982.

Michieka, Esther Nyabonyi. *An Investigation of the Causes of Pupil Drop-Out in Primary Schools in Kisii District of Kenya.* 1983.

Mohamed, Ibrahim Jeylani. *Investigation of Problems of Implementing Curriculum in Primary Schools in Somalia.* 1983.

Mukhalu, Francis. *Techniques and Strategies of Improving the Supervision, Assessment, and Evaluation of the Competence of Student Teachers in the Kenya Primary Teachers' Training Colleges.* 1982.

Mutiso, Margaret A. *Towards Determining and Developing an Appropriate Video Programme for In-Service Training of Primary School Teachers in Kenya.* 1982.

Mutsune, M. *Relationship Between Theory and Practical Biology at "A" Level in Kenya Secondary Schools.* 1983.

Nguchu, Ruth Rukunga. *The Extent to Which Radio is Used in Teaching of Home Science in Urban Primary Schools in Kenya.* 1981.

Njeremani, Rodah D. *An Examination of the Suitability of Primary Teachers' College Graduates as Primary School Teachers in Kenya.* 1982.

Obiero, On'gan'ga O. *An Evaluation of the Effectiveness of Radio Programmes in Teaching English Language to Class Six Pupils in Primary Schools in South Nyanza, Kenya.* 1982.

Ochola, J. *Relevance of Suggested Textbooks for the Teaching of New Chemistry Syllabus in Kenya Secondary Schools.* 1983.

Odede, Esther A. *The Role of the Teachers Advisory Centres in the Qualitative Improvement of Teacher Education in Kenya.* 1982.

Otewa, John O. *Factors Affecting the Teaching of Biology in Both Government and Harambee Secondary Schools in Kenya.* 1983.

Owiger, Agutu Owigar. *A Study of Attitudes of Teachers and Pupils Toward History Teaching by Radio in Nairobi Primary Schools.* 1981.

Rarieya, Marie J. *Pre-School Education in Kisumu.* 1983. (Kenya)

Waweru, Julius Macharia. *Social-Economic Background as an Influence Factor in Pupils' Achievement in Primary Schools in Embu District, Kenya.* 1982.

Wanyoike, E.N. *A Teacher Training Reading Methodology Manual in Kiswahili for Lower Primary Classes in Kenya.* 1982.

Were, Nereah. *An Examination of the Problems Relating to the*

Teaching of History in Secondary Schools in Kenya. 1982.

Worku, Shimeles. *The Implementation of Technical Education Curriculum in the Reorganized Secondary Schools in Addis Ababa.* 1981.

SOUTHERN AFRICA

Chabane, Charles Moeletsi. *Evaluation of Lesotho Primary Teachers' Guide for Mathematics.* 1980.

Chali, K. *Teacher Training for Curriculum Implementation In Zambia.* 1983.

Chimwenje, Dennis Danny. *Evaluation of Geography Teaching in Malawian Secondary Schools with Special Reference to the Need for Specific Objectives.* 1981.

Malama, Aaron. *The Teaching of English for Specific Purposes in Technical Education in Zambia.* 1982.

Matlhaka, Tselanngwe L. *Investigation of Training and Job Opportunities for Primary School Leavers in Mochudi, Botswana.* 1980.

Motha, Esness. *The Development of Instructional Units on Family Life Education for the Primary Teachers' Certificate in Swaziland.* 1981.

Msosa, Josuphite. *An Examination of the Suitability and Relevance of the Prescribed Textbooks for English Literature at Junior Certificate Level in Malawi Secondary Schools.* 1982.

Mundia, Namabanda W. *The Problems of Teaching and Learning the Mother Tongue as a Subject in Primary Schools of Zambia.* 1982.

Munungwe, Fidelis M. *The Use of English as a Medium of Instruction in the First Three Grades of Zambian Primary Education.* 1982.

Muyangana, Gideon M. *Investigation of Effects of Some Selected Methods for Improving the Performance of Slow Readers in Zambian Schools.* 1980.

Mwamba, Ignatious. *Essentials for Implementing Practical Subjects in Zambia Primary Schools.* 1983.

Nkamba, Simon C.H. *Development of Music Curriculum and Instructional Materials for Primary Schools in Zambia.* 1980.

Nxumalo, M.   *Curriculum Studies, Instructional Materials, Teacher Training Colleges in Swaziland.* 1983.

Pungwa, Lawrence. *Development of Social Studies Curriculum Content for Zambian Junior Secondary Schools.* 1982.

Ramothea, Leeto A. *Assessment of the Effectiveness of the Schools Educational Radio Broadcasting at Junior Secondary Level in Lesotho.* 1982.

Shaba, A.M.I. *An Examination of the Effectiveness of Science Educators in Teachers Colleges in Malawi.* 1981.

JOURNALS

The journals that are most likely to contain articles on African Education are listed below. They are organized into three categories. First, are those journals that are most prominent, second, are journals that often contain articles, and third, those that occasionally offer an article. Each category is listed in alphabetical order.

Most Prominent

Canadian and International Education
Comparative Education
Comparative Education Review
Compare
Convergence
Integrated Education
International Journal of Educational Development
International Review of Education Research
Journal of International and Comparative Education
Journal of Southern African Studies
Kenya Journal of Education
Perspectives in Education
Prospects International
South African Journal of Education Development
Zimbabwe Journal of Education

Often

Anthropology and Education Quarterly
International Education
Journal of Abstracts in International Media in ×
     Education and Educational Development
Journal of African Studies
Journal of Black Studies
Journal of Curriculum Studies Interchange
Journal of Moral Education
Journal of Negro Education
Muslim Educational Quarterly
Negro Educational Review

Occasionally

Adult Education
British Journal of Sociology of Education
Chronicle of Higher Education
Development in Education

Distance Education
Educational Forum
Educational Media International
Educational Review
Educational Studies
Education and Production
Education and Society
Harvard Educational Review
Higher Education
History of Education Quarterly
International Journal of Lifelong Education
International Journal of Science
International Social Science Journal
Journal of Educational Thought
Journal of General Education
Journal of Research and Educational Leadership
Journal of Special Education
Journal of Teacher Education
Journal of Thought
Oxford Review of Education
Phi Delta Kappan
Science Education
Social Education
Teachers College Record

INDEX